GATORS
GUTS,
& Glory

ADVENTURES ALONG THE FLORIDA TRAIL

GATORS GUTS, & *Glory*

ADVENTURES ALONG THE FLORIDA TRAIL

LAURALEE BLISS
"Blissful"

WhiteFire
Publishing

GATORS, GUTS, AND GLORY: ADVENTURES ALONG
THE FLORIDA TRAIL

Copyright © 2019, Lauralee Bliss

Cover design by Roseanna White Designs
Cover photo by Nancy Basque Frey

WhiteFire Publishing
13607 Bedford Rd NE
Cumberland, MD 21502

ISBNS: 978-1-946531-70-4 (print)
        978-1-946531-33-9 (digital)

*To Nancy, my big sister and a true servant of Christ.
I owe a debt of gratitude.*

*And we know that in all things
God works for the good of those
who love him, who have been called
according to his purpose.*

Romans 8:28 (NIV)

PART I

BEGINNINGS

*GREAT CYPRESS NATIONAL PRESERVE
TO THE HALFWAY POINT*

CHAPTER ONE

A MONUMENT TO SUCKING MUD

Is anyone out here?

There's been no water for miles, no semblance of humanity, and my water bag is dry. I am a lone wanderer on the Florida Trail, and things are getting desperate.

Water is normally everywhere, pouring out of faucets, filling rivers and streams and great oceans. One never misses anything so commonplace—until you don't have it. I look at my empty water bottles while my tongue runs over parched lips. Many of the streams listed in my guidebook are dried up. The sweltering Florida sun beats down, and my need for water after hiking many miles is getting critical. I must have some liquid refreshment soon, not only to ease the dryness in my throat that feels like sandpaper, but really, to prevent full-blown dehydration.

I lumber along, wondering what to do, when I look off to my left. Suddenly I spot a silvery pool glistening in the bright Florida sun. It's a pond of water, surrounded by a beach of black sand. *Water! Yes!* Heaven on earth. *Thank you, God.*

I need to leave the trail and walk out to the pool of

water, but that shouldn't be difficult. I've already done many things to reach water—hiking through tall grass, slogging across bogs and cypress domes while batting away palmettos in my face. The black sand looks pretty wet, so I elect to keep my backpack and shoes on grassy turf and don my Crocs—my favorite footwear for camp and water crossings (they have holes in them to drain out water). I pick up a water bag and small cup I use to collect the water from a natural source and gingerly make my way toward the pond. How lovely it looks. I can't wait.

I step onto the black sand. And sink. Rapidly. All the way up to my hip. It's not sand but a muddy trap known as sucking mud.

"No!" I yell. I try to pull out my leg but I'm stuck fast. I twist, attempting to maneuver out of this mucky stranglehold and finally drag my leg out, now covered in black slime. I step out with my other foot and meet the same fate. Mud all the way to my hip.

No, no. How am I going to get out of this? How am I going to get the water I need?

As a hiker I've been in lots of wacky situations. I've done over 6,000 miles on the Appalachian Trail in all kinds of weather and in wild terrain where I thought I'd lose my life. I'd been lost and stabbed on the Allegheny Trail in West Virginia. I'd been in a veritable wind tunnel and flooding rains along Vermont's Long Trail, not to mention my backpack falling off a cliff, but that's another story. I'd been attacked by the infamous Japanese hornet on the Foothills Trail of South Carolina where my leg swelled to twice its normal size. But I've never be caught in quicksand, i.e. sucking mud.

Memories of the classic movie *The Princess Bride* flash through my mind, of the hero and heroine caught in the depths of lightning sand and nearly suffocating. If I don't find a way out of here, I could very well be stuck for who knows how long, a permanent muddy monument to the rigors of the Florida Trail.

I force away the fear and turn to prayer, asking fast and furious for help from above. There is no one else out here but God, and He has been with me through thick and thin. Though right now I'm in a situation as thick as mud. I think of how often God has dispatched mighty angels to help in my time of need as I wander these many trails. I wonder if the angels pull straws in heaven to see who is responsible for helping Blissful the Hiker out of her latest predicament. Seriously though, I consider how much angels have taken care of little ol' me, involved in some crazy stunt while hiking a trail. And here I am in another pickle jar, stuck fast in the mud. I've never been through anything like this before. But then again…I've never done anything like this before, either. Nothing is normal out here. And maybe that's a good thing. A backpacking trip should never be boring.

Welcome to "Adventures along the Florida Trail." You will never be the same.

CHAPTER TWO

THE ADVENTURE IS BORN

There's nothing like a return journey on the trail of my dreams, and here I am in late March, hiking for a third time along a section of the Appalachian Trail from the Great Smoky Mountains to Spivey Gap in Tennessee. I've been out a week in nearly every kind of weather. In the Great Smokies, foot-high snowdrifts turn to ice when melted by freak rain. Ice then turns to slush that soaks through trail shoes and makes the way slippery. Farther down the trail, slush turns to mud that grabs hold of feet like mini pools of quicksand, sucking off trail shoes. Hitting the town of Hot Springs to dry out, clean up, and eat is now on the hiker menu.

I arrive at the Laughing Heart Hiker Hostel with soaked gear and soaked feet from all the precipitation the sky has dished out. The friendly hosts greet me and offer me a real bed while pointing out the major hiker necessities like the washer and dryer and the showers. Yes, there is wondrous scenery and friends on a trail, but oh, how I cherish the comforts of civilization in the feel of clean clothes, a clean self, a bed, and lots of food.

Once my basic needs are met, I wander about the hostel, looking around the sitting room with books lining the shelves and a hiker box brimming with leftover food in Ziploc bags and heavy gear no one would ever want to haul. I then examine the posters decorating the walls. One in particular draws my interest: a full-length map of the Florida Trail. I gaze at it intently, from its beginning in the Big Cypress Swamp, winding its way some 1,100 miles north and west across the Panhandle to Pensacola Beach and its northern terminus at Fort Pickens on the Gulf Islands National Seashore. In the past I spent a good deal of time in Florida—visiting relatives and scouring the famous landmarks of beaches, historical sites, tourist attractions, and orange groves. But hiking a trail in Florida is something I never considered. There are also rumors of the challenge found in the Florida Trail's beginning— that is, trudging for days in knee-deep water through a swamp. After hiking in slush on this Appalachian Trail venture, I shake my head at the thought of unending wet feet with a pack on my back and no place to rest. I'm enduring enough of it on this trek.

The caretaker of the hostel—trail name[1] "Chuck Norris"—now ventures forward as I continue to look over the poster. "So is the Florida Trail difficult?" I ask him.

"No, not really."

Oh yeah? What about the swamp things? Walking in all that water—how can a hiker possibly survive such an ordeal? "I know you have to go through water for several days," I say to Chuck Norris. "Your shoes must get ruined as well as your feet. What do you do?" I'm thinking of my wet feet when I arrived here and how uncomfortable it made me feel.

---

[1] Trail names are a unique aspect of the trail community. It's a name either given to you or one you call yourself to replace your real name. In most instances it represents something interesting about you or an interest you have.

He shrugs. "It's quite easy. You just wear a pair of old shoes through the swamp. When you get out of the swamp, you throw away the old shoes and have a new pair waiting for you."

Sounds logical enough. But I still can't wrap my mind around the idea of actually wading through deep water with no place to rest one's weary self. And then the isolation where no living thing can be found but for the alligators and water moccasins. You have to be crazy to even consider it. And that's that.

Anyway, a trail in a swamp is not my idea of the Sunshine State. Florida had been a vacation mecca of mine for years, especially when my parents used to rent a condo in Largo every winter. Along the Florida coast there's plenty to do. I loved wandering up the western coast to the quaint Greek village of Tarpon Springs where one can take a boat ride to learn about harvesting sponges from the deep, indulge in buttery baklava at a Greek bakery, or browse the many shops all filled with the same items for sale—sponges of every shape and size. Then there's Homosassa Springs with its boat ride through the bogs and wildlife exhibits. Farther down the coast is Sanibel Island, known for its seashells, and Fort Myers with the winter homes of neighboring inventors Henry Ford and Thomas Edison. Not to mention the beaches that frame a subdued Gulf of Mexico. On the east coast is the great Atlantic Ocean with its mighty waves and pristine beaches, and the Kennedy Space Center that has seen man journey to the moon and the International Space Station. There are sprawling beach resorts and a pool in everyone's backyard. And of course who can forget Orlando—home to orange groves, Walt Disney World and the famous Cinderella's castle, the whales and penguins in Sea World, and other high-priced amusements. Those are my images of Florida.

Now I'm trying to imagine Florida by trail, wandering

through the heart of a state where nothing I attribute to Florida even exists. In fact, what *does* exist in the Florida wilderness?

I grab a pamphlet about the trail from a stack of literature in the hostel's library and take it back to my room. I scan the map to find the dots of a trail meandering through a swamp, around a humungous lake, and through the middle of the state where hardly any civilization abounds. Wilderness in my eyes is what I hiked for so many miles on my treks along the Appalachian Trail, the Long Trail of Vermont, and the Foothills Trail of South Carolina. Trees. Mountain summits. Streams. Maybe the Florida wilderness is still hardwoods and streams and wildlife, all set in flatland, flanked by water on either side. And of course, the swamps of the Everglades.

I set the brochure aside. For now this trail is just a passing interest. I'm walking the trails I know best—those that traverse mountain ranges, cross streams playing over moss-covered rocks, meander through hardwoods and spruce, and deliver stunning views and a great finish. All the things that have come from ten years of wandering in eastern woodlands on a nicely graded pathway marked by white blazes, called the Appalachian Trail. It's all I've ever known. I will never tackle anything else, let alone something as wild and strange as the Florida Trail.

Never say never.

* . * . *

A few years later I take off to hike a relatively unknown long-distance trail in West Virginia called the Allegheny Trail.[2] This is the first time I'll be gone for several weeks on a 330-mile wander that is not the Appalachian Trail. I

---

[2] For information, maps and guidebook about the Allegheny Trail, visit the West Virginia Scenic Trails Association website: www.wvscenictrails. org

have no idea what to expect except that it's a yellow-blazed footpath wandering through the Monongahela National Forest of West Virginia, over mountains, into valleys, and through towns. It's also a trail that no one knows exists. To me, that's a bonus. I can be a forerunner, so to speak, blazing paths with a pioneer spirit. And yes, undergoing the testing that's part of a pioneer's journey into the vast unknown. Little did I realize, but my journey along the Allegheny Trail would ready me for future adventures.

One big difference about hiking the Allegheny Trail is the roadwalking. All of the Appalachian Trail, except for bits here and there, has been carefully moved off roads and onto land easements of woods and fields for that wilderness feel. But on parts of the Allegheny Trail, it's pure rambling on country roads. When you're in the woods, you feel isolated and therefore protected. Not so on a roadwalk with cars zipping by and drivers witnessing someone lumbering along carrying a backpack. On one roadwalk there's only a narrow strip of shoulder to hike on with semi-trucks zipping by at fifty-five miles-per-hour. You need to be aware of your surroundings at all times. And no wearing earbuds, jazzing with the music.

Case in point. During one of my many roadwalks on the Allegheny Trail, a driver in a van pulls up beside me. The mere act itself is unnerving. He then opens the window and thrusts out his hand. I step back to see his calloused fingers holding a twenty dollar bill. "Here you go," he says.

I stare at the money in stunned amazement before politely informing him I'm okay, not down on my luck or homeless. I'm out walking a trail.

No matter. Again he tries to give it to me, to which I adamantly refuse. Instead I suggest he give it to someone in need. The man reluctantly drives off. When I mention the event on social media, some thought I should have accepted the gesture and then pass it forward to others.

In hindsight, maybe I should have. For me personally, I'm amazed that folks think someone carrying a backpack is down on their luck and in great need. I have all that I need when I tackle a trail. The backpack is my home, the trail a means to an end, the journey a life-changing experience of drawing closer to God and His creation. But I will say that this situation is a first for me, and interestingly enough, will not be my last.

The second major eye-opener in hiking the Allegheny Trail is the effort it takes to simply follow the trail. Whereas I'm used to the familiar white rectangular blaze neatly painted on trees along the Appalachian Trail to guide my every step, the blazes on the Allegheny Trail are few and far between. Trees on the Allegheny Trail are marked by rectangular yellow blazes, if done correctly. In hindsight I should've brushed up on navigation skills. I must rely on maps of the trail and descriptions in a very old guidebook with updates to the guidebook printed on twenty other pages. Thankfully the trail maps prove fairly accurate. I try to pay close attention to the blazing when I do find it. Some sections of the Allegheny Trail are blazed better than others. Some blazing amounts to faint splotches of dying yellow on a tree. At times there are no blazes at all but just a trail trace to follow. It didn't take long for me to become fairly adept at following a faint trail that only a herd of deer may have used. I look for any bit of paint still lingering on tree bark that has not been stripped off by an animal or by the elements. I have become a navigator of the woods.

But several times I did lose the trail. There I am, stuck on some mountaintop, knowing the trail is ready to turn and head via switchbacks to the valley below. If I miss the turn-off, I could be wandering around for a long time, and no one would know where to find me. I will become a MHA—Missing Hiker in Action.

In these situations, the appropriate lyrics to a song

would come to mind—and one I sing often to calm my fear. "Help Me Find It" by Sidewalk Prophets. I sing it a lot, using my own words too. "Help me find it, God. Help me find this trail, a blaze, anything! Help me not get lost. Help me stay calm. Help me." It becomes my rallying cry to this elusive trail. It's a time to build up faith when every part of you wants to give in to fear and uncertainty. I search for any sign of a trail or blaze, continuing to murmur, "Help me find it." I look over the contour lines on my trusty map to see the trail veering away from the mountain just before the summit. From this I deduce where to go and at last locate a yellow blaze and the trail. I'm learning to get myself out of sticky situations by using the brain God gave me, an outdated map, and that still, small Voice directing my path.

Besides the blazing, the Allegheny Trail is not beautifully maintained in its entirety like the Appalachian Trail. In their spare time a few hardworking volunteer maintainers care for this 330-mile path. Some areas are better maintained than others. In places there are large blowdowns blocking the trail, requiring you to go off trail around the fallen tree and somehow find your way back to the trail trace—a nearly impossible task if it's foggy. In one section of the trail atop a place called Shaker Mountain, a friendly maintainer warned me of a quarter mile laced with thorns and I better have bandages. I thought he must be exaggerating. When I reach the area, all I can think of is the prince in *Sleeping Beauty,* fighting his way through thick thorns to reach the castle. How I wish I had a machete as I plunge into the thorns that tear at my backpack, my clothes, and my skin. When I arrive at camp that night, my arms and legs are covered in tracks made by the thorns, some angry red streaks, others bleeding, all of it painful. I'm the victim of a battle waged against a trail. As I lay there in my tent after applying antibiotic ointment, the cuts screaming in vengeance, I wonder what on earth is motivating me to endure such trials. No one cares. None of this makes sense. Why put myself through it? "Weeping [from cuts] may endure for the night, but joy comes in the morning" (Psalm 30:5). The next morning, a pretty grove of pine trees with streams of sunlight piercing through the fog greets me. I'm learning to cope with the rigors of a walk that make the beauty of wilderness appear even more stunning—with its vistas and flowing streams and the grandeur of Blackwater Falls. I'm becoming not just a hiker but a pioneer, working through the trials of the wilderness where there may or may not be a trail to follow. Most of all, I'm becoming a determined adventurer who refuses to let thorns or faded pathways or fear deprive me of a journey.

A few days later I face another obstacle by way of stepping on a limb. The sharp end of the stick flies up and stabs me in the left lower leg. Bleeding profusely and with some kind of whitish flesh showing, I shiver, thinking it's a tendon or something. I decide to leave the trail and have it doctored. Thankfully in a week the wound heals nicely, and I'm back out there though forever sporting a deep scar on my lower leg as a medal for hiking the Allegheny Trail. A few days later I sprain my ankle in a hole after wandering over yet another blowdown. I worry this will do me in. But I take medicine, wrap the ankle in an elastic bandage, and continue on, determined not to let this trail beat me to an almost bloody pulp.

Even on my final day on the Allegheny Trail, beset with foggy, rainy weather, I spend it trying to locate faded blazes and end up lost in the thick mist, all the time hiking without food. Yes, I had inadvertently forgotten my food bag that day in the car. Just completing this forsaken trail is taking me to the brink of everything I thought I knew about hiking. But to my relief, God once more provides a way out as I spot several apple trees with fruit dangling from the branches. And somehow the blazes appear out of the thick fog to guide my way out of there, all the way to the finish line where the Allegheny trail unites with the Appalachian Trail.

I did it. I hiked the entire Allegheny Trail. The completion feels sweet in many ways, thinking of all I had endured, from thorns to a tree stabbing, from an ankle injury to food deprivation and losing my way, all to a glorious conclusion.

I arrive home diced and spliced but with a mental hardiness that gives me the confidence I need to go for experiences well out of my comfort range. For months after the Allegheny Trail, I wonder why God has led me on a trail through the wilds of West Virginia that no one cares about, let alone me. I wondered what the experience would do to me as a hiker and as a Christian. I wonder how this time of encountering the unexpected and finding oneself lost and in trouble would be used for a higher purpose. It's done something in me, that's for sure. It's made me a scarred adventurer. Maybe that's all it's supposed to do. Or is this preparing me for things yet to be played out?

* \. * \. *

A year later I find myself interested in other long-distance trails out there, and the idea of hiking the Florida Trail re-enters the picture from a seed planted long ago at a hostel in Hot Springs. Completing the journey on the Allegheny Trail changed me in many ways. The time has come to expand the learning to new horizons and seek new and exciting adventures, like the Florida Trail. Even if its beginning involves trekking through swamp water. I'd already been through a lot on the Allegheny Trail. The thorns didn't stop me, though they tried. The stick stabbed me, but I survived. The ankle gave out, but it healed. How much more damage can a few days walking in swamp water do? What's another adventure to add to life's list?

And so I begin some preliminary research into the Florida Trail. I join online groups to chat about the adventure and discover needed information. I start the wheel slowly rolling down the trail, so to speak. This is not a trail I longed to do, like the Appalachian Trail, which I dreamt of for thirty years before I accomplished it. But the Florida Trail is something I am destined to do.

Why?

Only time will tell.

CHAPTER THREE

On Your Mark,
Get Set,
GO!

I watch my husband Steve, trail name "Papa Bliss," look over the data, and in particular, the elevation profile of the Florida Trail. A smile forms on his rough face, encircled by a salt and pepper-colored beard. "No elevation gain?" he says. "No mountains to climb? Great! I can keep up with you then. Sure, I'll go."

I'm all smiles at the good news. I believe we're supposed to hike this crazy thing called the Florida Trail. Unlike convincing my husband many years ago that hiking the Appalachian Trail was a good idea—which had taken months—this is easy. He's used to me traipsing about as a solo adventurer while he's the guy who helps out when he can. Many times he's met me on the Appalachian Trail both north and south to resupply me or take care of issues. He did it during the Allegheny Trail and assisted me several times—first at Blackwater Falls State Park to resupply my food, second, to rescue me near Cass after the limb pierced my leg. He even drove halfway with a friend toward South Carolina to help transport me home after my leg swelled to twice its size from a Japanese hornet sting on the Foothills Trail. He's also been there when I accomplished many of my trail goals—like finishing my southbound Appalachian Trail hike at Harper's Ferry and the Allegheny Trail when I nearly collapsed from lack of food (and thankfully he had plenty tucked away in his daypack). So to hear he's interested in accompanying me on the first part of the Florida Trail, I'm all smiles.

During the planning phase, I quickly learn a flat trail doesn't mean there aren't inherent challenges like any other backpacking venture. To educate myself on what to expect, I join a Florida Trail hiking group on Facebook. Through the posts, I discover there's more to this wander than meets the eye. Like the very beginning, where hikers talk of going a mile an hour through the swamp water, littered with limestone holes and other impediments. Then the possible dangers in certain areas around Lake Okeechobee, for which they advocate not going alone. I realize from these conversations that a hiking buddy is necessary, and Papa Bliss's willingness to come along solves some major issues. Normally I strike out on my own when it comes to trails. I like to keep a certain pace, stop where I want, sleep when I want, etc. But it can get lonely out there, and with the observations I'm gathering about the trail dangers, a buddy to traipse through swamp water with me and make sure the boogeyman doesn't get me sounds like good and godly wisdom.

Another way of gathering wisdom is to hear directly from those older and wiser who have actually hiked the Florida Trail. For this I venture to the ALDHA, or the Appalachian Long Distance Hikers Association[3] annual "Gathering" where hikers do as the word says—gather to discuss trails and make new friends. I'm hoping this event will provide me with open doors to talk about my goal of hiking the Florida Trail. I run into a fellow hiker

---

[3] To find out more about ALDHA check out aldha.org

named Chase who did the trail a few years ago and begin asking questions. Suddenly I hear a woman answering the questions I'm posing from her grassy spot on a hillside. I don't think much about it until I discover Sandra is one of two authors who penned a guidebook for the Florida Trail. While I want to pick her brain for that vast wealth of knowledge, I know she has other things to do. But I do purchase the guide to help with the planning. I still find time to talk at length with another hiker, Tom, who has also done the trail and reiterates the one mile an hour speed in swamp walking to avoid limestone holes, which he says *does* take that long, even as I try to envision hiking at a snail's pace. He also describes how bad the mosquitoes can get and insists I must be in my tent no later than dusk and not arise until dawn. It's interesting to hear the advice of hikers while trying to envision what they're saying when I'm not out there yet. I wonder if the stories are exaggerated for effect, even though I still plan to wear old shoes and bring the bug netting. I guess I'll find out.

Motivated by these great contacts and my newly purchased trail guide, I throw myself into preparations. I plan for summer-like conditions, despite leaving for the hike in mid-December. Though I'm not going to the beach (sigh) or eating Greek food at Tarpon Springs (double sigh), I'm still going to Florida where it's warm. My clothing includes pants that zip off to convert to shorts, two t-shirts, one long sleeve shirt, a pair of leggings, a hat, a fleece pullover, a rain jacket, a wind jacket, some underwear, and four pairs of socks. I refuse to skimp on socks, particularly as I'm told your feet *will* get wet in many areas. Sort of like the ominous warning posted at an amusement park for the Whitewater Canyon ride. You *will* get wet on this ride! And going on these kinds of rides and experiencing it for myself, I know warnings should be heeded.

I tuck in a head net for the bugs, a baseball cap for the sun, a rain hat, and sunglasses. The rest of my gear is typical backpacking gear for sleeping and eating. I also make sure to have sunscreen and good bug repellent. And of course the ever important first aid kit. I hear the horror stories from hikers of unforgiving blisters from feet soaked in swamp water for days and then exposed to sandy roadwalks after that. It's a diabolical duo that can spell a mess for feet not used to the rigors of a trail. I buy new trail runners to have on hand after the swamp waltz is over. I also decide to do something new for this trail and purchase the Florida Trail map app for my cell phone. I've never used a map app before—I've usually relied on paper maps. So doing it this way will be new and different, and why not? It goes hand in hand with the idea of a new and different hike.

Next I spend time researching the trail and discover things I never thought I'd need to worry about. Like alligators lurking in the water sources. Water is the hiker's mainstay on a trail. Without it, you don't go anywhere fast. Now I'm warned in the guidebook *not* to fetch water at dusk lest the alligator mistake you for a deer. I can imagine the large reptile sneaking up to where I'm gathering water for the night, ready to chomp off my hand. Or if I'm leaning over, I can see the creature biting some other unmentionable part. It's kind of scary. In some ways I'm used to wildlife, having worked in Shenandoah National Park five years with black bears galore. I saw upward of forty to fifty bears a season. I had a bear chomp on my tent and charge me. I'm used to their antics. But alligators? Not in my neck of the woods. I imagine what could happen, like a vision from *Peter Pan* where the big crocodile, who's already tasted a timepiece and a hand, nonchalantly comes to finish off Captain Hook piecemeal. Not really a picture one should be envisioning when getting ready to descend into gatorland.

I forgo Disney's interpretations and stick to a formal gator review online, as I once did with black bear encounters. I read how it's better to approach an alligator from behind rather than the front. They are usually timid unless they develop fearlessness from humans feeding them. Why anyone would want to feed an alligator goes beyond my understanding. Gators are also motion sensitive. Striking the ground with hiking poles, for instance, will alert them to your presence. For the most part they are timid, doing their own thing in life as are most creatures. I hope they play shy for me, especially when I'm fetching water from a pond or river. I do not want to be mistaken for dinner.

I now read in the guidebook about poisonous plants that hikers can encounter, including poisonous trees. The tree, appropriately called poisonwood, contains a much higher percentage of the toxin urushiol that causes the itchy, blistering rash of misery we attribute to poison ivy. I'd never heard of a lethal tree that can wreak havoc if you brush up against it. I go online and see pictures of the leaves and the weeping on the tree trunks that looks like something out of a horror flick. No one hailing from the north would ever consider the existence of a poisonous tree. But hiking in Florida, as I'm about to find out, will be a different experience altogether. And poisonwood is another item to add to the ever-growing list of new things I might encounter, leading me to wonder...*what* am I getting myself into?

On any hike, a good guidebook helps with logistics, campsites and resupplying food, and yes, pointing out such dangers as alligators mistaking you for a scrumptious evening dinner or poisonous trees that can make life miserable or even dangerous. *The Florida Trail Guide,* under the banner of Florida Hikes,[4] is my main resource

---

[4] The Florida Hikes website contains up-to-date information on the Florida Trail as well as the invaluable trail guide. http://floridahikes.com/

for helping me prepare for this venture. Besides the flora and fauna, I discover that permits are required for hiking and camping in certain locations along the trail. I work to secure the permits for the Big Cypress National Preserve, the Seminole Indian Reservation, and camping along the Kissimmee River. Later on will come the permits for the Panhandle area of the state such as the St. Marks National Wildlife Refuge and Eglin Air Force Base. I also join the Florida Trail Association,[5] as a membership is helpful when using the trail through private lands or hunt clubs to avoid any unpleasant situations. Not to mention that a membership helps the trail on the whole. I tend to be an organizer, so it's good to have the basics covered early, like the permits and membership and asking questions on hiker forums. I decide not to worry over unforeseeable situations, which one can't possible plan for anyway. Trusting that everything will work out somehow is the main ingredient in a life built on faith, and faith carries one along on the trail of adventure.

With the start of the journey slated for mid-December, Papa Bliss and I examine options for celebrating Christmas Day trailside. Not wishing to spend the holiday lounging beside a canal filled with agricultural runoff or sharing it with the mosquitoes and alligators, Papa investigates where we may be able to stay near Lake Okeechobee— the approximate area we should be in by December 24th. The Florida Trail splits around this large lake, allowing hikers to venture either west or east to fulfill the trail. I immediately head to an online hiker forum to determine which route is the best. It's all fairly confusing as portions of the trail are closed due to construction on the dam surrounding the lake, forcing hikers out onto the roads. After talking to several hikers, we determine that east

---

[5] The Florida Trail Association offers information, membership, and maps, and helps coordinate maintenance of the trail http://www.floridatrail.org/

seems best, not only for the lake views along the way but the better lodging options available for Christmas. We find an enticing prospect in a lakeside cottage rental not far from a town called Pahokee. It will still entail roadwalking, as part of the trail is closed while the Corps of Engineers work to build new pump stations and fortify the dams. But is seems the best plan, especially for finding a cute place to spend the holidays. Papa places the call, and we secure a reservation for December 24th and 25th. Of course that means we must make certain mileage to arrive at the cottage on time. But with zero elevation gain on the Florida Trail, that shouldn't be too difficult.

Next is planning food for a long-distance hike. We make several trips to stores to buy supplies for mail drops, which are boxes of supplies mailed to convenient places along the route. The table begins to fill with assorted granola bars, M&M candies that won't melt in the hot Florida sun, dried cherries, and lots of pasta and rice for dinners. We dry veggies and meats in our food dehydrator. Papa Bliss stocks up on turkey sausages. The first box will also contain new shoes for when we ditch our swampy ones after the four-day trek through the Big Cypress National Preserve. Other boxes contain food for several days when the ability to buy food is sparse or nonexistent. It's a challenge trying to figure out the mileage between mail drops and the availability of towns for supplies. Two drops end up fairly spread out, meaning my pack will be loaded down with weight, but it can't be helped.

Everything appears to be falling into place for this grand adventure, though I still struggle with nagging doubt, wondering if I'm meant to hike this trail. I've had other trips postponed or cancelled in the past—for a family emergency, a wounded limb, a disruptive illness. It takes faith with all these preparations of buying food and mailing boxes, not knowing if the hike will actually take place. Especially on a trip where the unknown far outweighs the known. I've dealt in mountainside trails, through hills and dales, across streams and upward to lofty summits overlooking the valley below. The Florida Trail is in a class by itself. Few hikers have tackled the whole thing. I have never hiked in a swamp, among cypress trees, in prairies and wetlands, by gators and poisonous trees. I can't help having an element of anxiety. At least I have Papa Bliss to help me navigate the first two weeks before I strike out on my own. A flat trail should also minimize many of the physical issues one might face and provide for smooth sailing, i.e. hiking.

A few final tasks remain before undertaking this hike, like clearing the calendar of work and appointments. The days fill with things I was expecting to do before this trip became a reality. Like a contracted story due in to my publisher in the middle of the hike, on which I write furiously to get it done. And then there's one other item on the calendar.

Eye surgery.

Before the Florida Trail became a reality, I had undergone various tests on a rare cataract that formed in my right eye over the summer. Now the doctor wants to replace the lens, and I'm nervous how the surgery and its aftermath will gel with plans for the Florida Trail. So far the date for the surgery fits in, as does the follow-up. Until I get some bad news. The doctor has sprained her hand and can't operate. The surgery is moved back two weeks.

Yikes. Talk about cutting it close to the starting date of our hike. But I go ahead with the surgery, sporting the eye patch like Long John Silver. During my post-surgical visit, the doctor informs me I need to return in three weeks to recheck the eye. That falls smack dab in the middle of lumbering through palms and swamps on the Florida Trail. I hate to cut the trip short and now inform the doctor I'm a long-distance hiker planning to do this trail thing as part of an adventure bucket list. I don't go into the fact that a lot of sweat has already been poured into the planning of this trip, though I'm sure my expression reveals it.

She looks at me, looks at the schedule, and then says, "Okay. We'll see you in late January."

Relief pours over me. All the pieces to this grand puzzle are falling into place. God's traffic light is shining green to proceed. Even though my eyesight is blurry and I'll need to use two different bottles of eye drops in the middle of a hike, I'm squeaking by in the health department, and a squeak is all one needs.

Before leaving home, we celebrate an early Christmas while friends on social media puzzle over our video of the early gift exchange. This year will be unlike any other. We will spend the real Christmas Day in Florida, in the midst of a major hike. There's a time and season for everything under the hot Florida sun, and this is the year.

We line up the sitter for the dogs, I send in my contracted writing project to the editor, and I close down e-mail lists and other business. I make one final check of our gear and other items, as we will have the car in spots along the way for resupplying. Everything is packed and ready for a sixteen-hour road trip that will put us on the trail December 16th at the Big Cypress National Preserve— the trail's southern terminus.

I bid farewell to our dogs and my home sparsely decorated with a few Christmas lights to remind me that this is still the holiday season. A sixteen-hour trip is a marathon driving day, and we have given ourselves no wiggle room for the start date. But the drive goes smoothly, and we spend the night in Fort Pierce. On December 16th we drive west toward the city of Okeechobee, which we will hike to on our journey, and onward to the Everglades and the start of our grand adventure.

I'm glad I don't know the future, like what's in store for us on this hike. I don't think I would've gone if I did. But I refuse to shirk a challenge either, even if the challenge appears to surpass human endurance. Many times it goes beyond what we think to the supernatural. Or the miraculous. I'm not kidding myself. I'll need all the miracles God has put aside in His great storehouse to accomplish this trail.

CHAPTER FOUR

IN THE BEGINNING—THE SWAMP THING AND SUCH

BIG CYPRESS NATIONAL PRESERVE

"This map is not right," Papa Bliss complains.

We're lost already and have yet to set foot on the Florida Trail. We're stashing water caches along a portion of the trail that meanders by canals where the water is polluted with pesticides and agricultural run-off and inhabited by alligators of various sizes and temperaments. We plan to hike to this area in about five days, and Papa Bliss has figured out where we need to put the water for our hiking needs. But it's taking much longer than anticipated. The trail map on our phone doesn't match the handwritten map in the trail guide. Our eleven A.M. start time at the southern terminus of the Florida Trail is moved back. I'm trying not to let frustration rob me of peace, which is easier said than done. I must embrace the hiker beatitude of *Blessed are the flexible*. I like to plan everything out to a tee, but I ought to know, after several hiking experiences, the first thing a hiker should do on day one is throw out the plan. I will learn the hard way about ditching a plan and dealing with the anxiety of it. I just wish we didn't have a reservation for December 24th at a seaside bungalow, necessitating that we keep to some kind of schedule.

After figuring out the water caches, we finally arrive late to the Big Cypress National Preserve. It boasts the attractive Oasis Visitor Center with displays and information and its own alligator inhabiting a nearby canal. Before officially hitting the trail, we decide to seek out the friendly ranger inside the visitor center to ask a few questions about backpacking in the swamp. Some of his answers are not what we expect. Like descriptions of waist deep water and gators and water moccasins swimming on by. But he also talks about camping areas with picnic tables and firepits, which sound like nice stops. We must also wear blaze orange because it's hunting season. Afterward I head for the restroom for one final foray into modern convenience. Inside, the crisp linoleum and sinks are smeared with black mud as if someone has tried to rid themselves of the Florida Trail experience. That alone is an ominous sign of what's to come. I think about the conversations with hikers about walking in the swamp, and I take a deep breath. This is going to be interesting.

We return to the car to recheck our backpacks, fill our bottles with potable water (the last of its kind for a while), and ready ourselves to head out with great expectation for the first day's journey into the unknown. Opposite the visitor center is a large rock bearing the southern terminus marker for the Florida Trail and a great place to take the first of many photos to come. A logbook is also available to sign in with our thoughts about this momentous day. We walk past the ranger giving his afternoon talk about the park's native alligator, and I overhear a few things he's describing, like their size and what they eat and their temperament. If I do come across a gator, who moves first? I pray whenever we do meet, the gator is not hungry.

We then spy for the first time the bright orange blaze

that marks the Florida Trail, along with a very nice National Scenic Trail sign. And so it begins.

The start of the Florida Trail at Big Cypress National Preserve

We haven't been hiking long when Papa Bliss takes a flying leap backward. "Alligator!"

I stop dead in my tracks. He's seen one already! Wow! I gingerly hike up to meet him and there it is, staring at us from the brush. An alligator. Except...it's not real. We both groan loudly before Papa Bliss hugs the gator statue while I take a picture. It's an interesting welcome to the Big Cypress Swamp.

Pleasant, warm sunshine greets the day as we hike along, happy to finally be on the trail. We cross over many swamp buggy roads, named for the swamp buggies or vehicles with mega donuts for wheels that can navigate through mud and water. In the distance we hear gunshots from the hunters and quickly don our neon orange hats for visibility. I'm glad I'm also wearing my neon green shirt as the sounds are a bit nerve-racking. We walk through grass and see tall trees reaching to the horizon, much like a scene from an African safari. I half expect to round a bend and find an elephant or lion. It is certainly different from the thick woodlands back home.

The weather in Florida has been dry the past few weeks, so the trail, normally teeming with water here and there, is mainly a muddy mess. *This isn't so bad*, I decide. Even with all the hype I'd heard of the mile an hour progress, the worry seems premature.

We stop to drink water and eat a granola bar, noting how different the terrain is from any we have hiked in before. Papa Bliss also points out that in the warm weather, we are rapidly consuming our water supply and will need to fill up before we reach camp. Finding water in the dry sections of the Big Cypress Preserve can be interesting. There are no streams flowing down a mountain. The elevation here is roughly twenty feet, give or take. One must find a grove of cypress trees of which the varying tree heights form a dome-like configuration called a cypress dome. In the center of this dome of trees is a naturally occurring hole (the ranger called it a gator hole) with water in it. I've seen a few of these cypress tree domes on the horizon, and there's one to our west. Unfortunately to get to the dome, we must cross a muddy bog teeming with cypress and some kind of strange nodules poking out of the ground. These nodes of different sizes are called cypress knees and come from the roots of cypress trees. They serve no real function except they are fascinating to look at and can also cause injury if you accidentally stub a toe or trip over one of them. One must keep a careful eye to the ground when in a cypress knee area.

Slowly we make our way to the cypress dome through the mud and knobby cypress knees to find a dingy green pool of water. I try to scoop out water without also collecting the green slimy flakes that can easily clog a water filter. I can't help but get swamp things of different shapes and sizes along with the water. The water will now need to be strained before we can filter it. Sigh.

We return to the trail, navigating around the muddy areas wherever possible. Soon we arrive at a campsite noted by a sign but minus the table and firepit promised by the ranger. The campsite is well short of where I'd planned to be tonight, but that can't be helped. The late start meant a shorter-mile day, so here we are. We strain the swamp things out of the water through a bandana and then filter it, but all that work doesn't seem to help the indescribable taste, which I guess is the taste of a swamp.

There are plenty of trees for Papa to string up his hammock, and I find a flat spot to set up my tent. All around us we hear strange bird chatter. By six P.M. darkness falls and the insects arrive but far fewer in number than what I'd been expecting. Inside my tent I take stock of the miles we need to accomplish the next day to make our goal of Oak Hill camp—the first campsite located in the water section of the trail. It will require a long fifteen-mile day to get there. I believe we can do it, especially if we want a day to relax once we exit the area at the Seminole Reservation. It usually takes a good day after the swamp to dry out wet feet and prevent blisters, so we have planned a day off there.

The next morning I awake to find my tent heavily saturated with dew—a phenomenon I will need to get used to in Florida's humidity. The temperatures begin to climb as we head out to discover we're stiff and sore from our first day on the trail. The wild things are coming to greet us this day. Papa sights a bobcat. Deer prance through the grass. The deer of Florida are a much smaller version of their Virginia cousins but still with the telltale white flag of their tails. It's nice to know there are living things out here besides two grubby hikers. Except for hearing gunshots, we have not seen anyone.

The trail turns boggy and muddy in many areas, slowing

our progress. Papa slips and slides and finds his hip is bothering him. The sun beats down with equal intensity to match the mood of the trail, and we drink down our swamp water quicker than expected. With the pace we are setting and the frequent stops, I start to realize pretty quickly we are *not* going to reach our intended goal of fifteen miles today.

Resting in a small dry area that we manage to locate in the middle of the mud, I look over the trail guide. If we don't make the miles, we're in real danger of not making the cottage we have rented for Christmas. I tell Papa my concerns. From his viewpoint, the rental house is not the current issue. He is more interested in trying to make it to the next rest stop, with hurting muscles, a possible pulled groin, and the weight of his backpack where he is carting an extra pound of munchies in the side pockets. I sense the anxiety building within me and wonder what to do. I'm staring at one of the major laws of hiking—throw out the plans after day one and improvise.

I hike ahead of Papa to reach Thirteen Mile Camp, once more without any table or firepit. I wonder now if the ranger at the Oasis Visitor Center ever ventured out to see these campsites. Looking at my empty water bottles, I know Papa's must be dry too as he guzzles down much more than me. It could also be why I hear a groan in the distance as he deals with the difficulties. To make matters more uncertain, this campsite is also home to a patch of those poisonous trees I once read about. Brushing up against one of them could mean the brush of itchy torture. I now look at each tree warily and wonder if it's poisonous. I stay far away from anything and everything green.

What am I doing out here? This is crazy. We could be at some pristine beach by the ocean, taking a dip, relaxing with an iced tea, laughing away. *Papa would love that*, I think as I hear another distant groan. Or we could be back home, enjoying the spirit of the Christmas season in lights, carols, and baking my favorite Christmas cookie, Mexican Wedding Cakes.

But no. We are in Swampland, USA, dehydrated and surrounded by poisonwood. This could be a great scenario for a reality television show or a new plot for a science fiction drama. Except I'm dealing with the reality of empty water bottles and the realization that I'd better hunt down some swamp water soon. I check the map on my phone to find that a cypress dome is located one-tenth of a mile northwest. I bargain with God that if by some miracle there is water in the middle of that dome, I will apologize to Papa Bliss for getting upset over our lack of progress and trust God with our plans, come what may.

I set out to find water, recalling the muddy bog we hiked through yesterday to find a water source. I remember passing a muddy bog just before stumbling into Thirteen Mile Camp and return to that same place. I see the cypress dome and head toward it, praying there's a golden ticket hidden in the vegetation. Sure enough, I stumble upon a large pond. I march right into the middle of the pond, shoes and all (they're already wet from the trail anyway) and gingerly gather water while avoiding the swamp things. I return to the camp in triumph, eager to present Papa with the gift of water. I expect appreciation and a smile.

When he arrives he grabs the water, slugs it down, and talks about how sore and hot and miserable things are out here. I'm wondering if hunger might also have something to do with the mood. Since we have water nearby, I decide to go ahead and cook an early dinner. We can then hike in the cool of the evening and hit a campsite just before we enter the real swampy part of the trail. Papa agrees after collapsing on the ground. I cook, and we eat macaroni and cheese and rest. We head out a while later and after about an hour of hiking, find a large, grassy area to set up camp and await the dawn of another interesting day in the Big Cypress National Preserve.

* . * . *

We're feeling better the next morning and that's a good thing, as next up is the notorious water crossing. After some barbed wire fencing that signals the end of dry land, inwardly I hope the trail has dried out. No such luck. We come upon an inky blackness, shimmering under the rays of sun, and the fun of sloshing through ankle to knee deep water for many miles begins. And yes, limestone holes lay hidden in the water. I use my poles to keep my balance and probe for those menacing obstacles that could sprain or break an ankle. I stop frequently to dig out the mud that builds up inside my shoes. If I don't, the muddy chunks press on tender areas of my saturated feet and cause pain.

The map app on my phone proves critical for staying on the "trail," if one can call it that, and finding places where we can exit the water into a "forest hammock" to rest. These hammocks are not the kind one envisions—of material strung up between trees. Hammocks in this case are clumps of oak, perched on high ground above water. I find one such spot where a tree has even fallen to provide a makeshift bench. I look at the time and realize at best we are hiking about 7/10 a mile an hour. It is a test of patience and perseverance in taking literally one step at a time. We come to the decision that Ivy Camp will be our destination for the night—named, unfortunately, for the poison ivy that has overtaken the island. Sigh.

We stop for lunch at Oak Hill Camp—which was supposed to be our camping area the night before. Collapsing here beside a gnarly oak, I realize quickly the idea of hiking fifteen miles through water could not have happened. It seems God is helping guide our decision-making, despite my personal itinerary. The pleasant spot

Blissful is up to her knees in swamp water!

is a small island jutting out of the surrounding swamp and provides a place to air out our wet and muddy feet. We peel off socks and shoes, and I find some skin peeling off my feet too. Looking around the site, I notice we aren't the only ones that have used this place for drying out feet, as hikers have inadvertently left behind muddy socks still hanging from tree branches. Eating the snacks Papa has hidden away, we feel refreshed, but there's still plenty of water to slog through before we reach Ivy Camp.

Returning to the trail of water, I decide not to dwell on my discomfort but concentrate on the things of nature that I see when hiking in a swamp. Like the unique flora that exists out here. Good-size cypress trees grow out of the murky water, draped with Spanish moss. Knobby cypress knees poke out to greet us. Papa Bliss is happy about those cypress knees jutting out of the water, as they provide a place to rest for a few moments. Sloshing through the deepest part of the swamp called the Black Lagoon, where the ranger told us it would be waist deep, the water only rises to our calves, and we're grateful. I take out my phone to garner that once-in-a-lifetime photo of us backpacking in a swamp with the telltale orange blaze of the Florida Trail painted on a cypress trunk. I'm settling into the routine of a swamp walk, the slow pace of it all, maintaining my balance using a hiking pole while scraping mud out of a shoe, and avoiding the limestone holes and cypress knees that try to trip me up. Life is okay, but it will get even better when I finally graduate out of this murky place. Except I still have one night to go.

Arriving late to Ivy Camp, we find the incredible trail maintainers have painstakingly cleaned out a good deal of poison ivy from the campsite. They should be awarded medals for:

1) clearing the camp of poison ivy and
2) dragging the equipment needed through knee-deep swamp water so they *could* clear the poison ivy.

We set up camp quickly as the sun begins to sink, and with it comes the insects flying in to pay us a visit. I head out to gather our evening water, finding it strange to walk down the bank and dip water out of the lagoon that serves as the trail and surrounds the entire island. I try to wash the mud out of my trail runners that have become like two-pound cement blocks with mud solidifying within the shoes' fibers. The mud is also causing the fabric to separate. My shoes are literally falling apart. Thank goodness for the advice of "Chuck Norris" long ago on the

Appalachian Trail when he suggested I have new shoes waiting for me at the end of the swamp. The ones I wear now will never be the same.

I study the guide for tomorrow's wander and find the trail should be much easier. We are nearing the end of the water section, then it's just a few miles to the rest area off Interstate 75. After that it's another ten miles on flat terrain to reach the Seminole Indian Reservation. For Papa's part, he is dealing with groin pain that hasn't let up in two days and is contemplating hitching a ride from the rest area to our car parked at the visitor center. I'm hoping to find him a ride through a list of names I have after I discover we have cell service in the midst of a swamp. I talk to a few people by cell phone but have no luck finding a ride.

We settle in for the night when Papa's cell phone suddenly goes off inside his hammock, startling us. To his amazement, a random couple heard of our predicament and now offers to meet Papa at the rest area and drive him back to our car parked at the Oasis Visitor Center. Papa is stunned how all this is working out. Right in the middle of a swamp, we are able to set up a ride for noon the next day. For me, it's an answer to a silent prayer. Like the time God led me to water at Camp Thirteen and has been with me throughout all my hiking adventures far and wide. I did pray that Papa Bliss would likewise experience God's hand on the journey. And he is starting to become a true believer of that scripture that says all things really do work out for those called to God's purposes. And I guess we can say He has called us, and me personally, to hike the Florida Trail.

Now with Papa taken care of, I realize I may be able to hike the full seventeen miles to the Seminole Reservation and make up for the lost miles spent swamping it out in the Big Cypress National Preserve. Despite my worry and watching plans disappear, by accomplishing this feat, we will still be on track for our Christmas holiday escape, if all goes well.

The next day dawns bright and sunny, mirroring our cheerfulness as we trek out of the water and onto dry land. I forge ahead, looking to the forest hammocks on the horizon and tall palm trees reaching to the skies, reminding me of some far off island in the Pacific. I meet up with Papa at Pine Island for a rest and foot drying session, thankful to be leaving this wet but interesting place. Not to say that my feet will be sad, but rather both feet and body and spirit will be very glad.

We exit the swamp onto a wide road used by the swamp buggies. It's now a short jaunt to the rest area for vehicles traveling the interstate known as Alligator Alley. I still have ten miles left to finish the day, but just getting to this point, having come through the swamp, feels like a tremendous accomplishment. At the rest area I take off my shoes to dry my feet, change out my socks, and sort through gear for Papa to take back to the car when his shuttle arrives. Once he picks up our car at the visitor center, he will meet me at the end of the day in the Seminole Indian Reservation. I will only carry what I need for the afternoon hike rather than all my backpacking gear—a technique commonly known as slackpacking. It will be a nice change after several days of slogging along with a full pack on my back. We buy some cold drinks out of the machine and eat some snacks. My only disappointment in the rest area is that the lovely ice cream vending machine is out of order. Sigh.

When I set out to finish the next ten miles of trail, I can't believe how light and airy I feel with just a daypack on my back. The trail in this section is still part of the Big Cypress National Preserve, but there is no water to wade through, only dirt roads paralleling an active canal. I'm not long on the trail when I pass a large blackish object resting right beside the trail. I suddenly come to a screeching halt and gasp. Lounging in the grass is a seven foot alligator! I'd walked right passed him and he nary moved a reptilian muscle. He seems frozen in place, even as I gingerly take out my cell phone to grab a picture. He couldn't care less I'm there, and that's a relief. It's also a good thing his snout is to the canal and his tail to the road—the safest way to pass a gator in the wild. So now I can officially say I've seen Florida's native son and survived with all extremities intact.

Florida's native son, or rather the back of him,
and the safest place for a hiker to pass quietly by

Above me, large birds swoop from tree to tree, calling to each other about the strange person trying to finish a very long hiking day. I see snowy white egrets and ibises and herons. This place is a proverbial wildlife park, serenaded by the occasional splash of gators flipping around in an attempt to get comfortable in their watery canal bed. Farther along I take a picture of two gators side by side, one of which has its head in the water as if they'd been in some kind of gator argument and he's hiding in shame. How I wish Papa Bliss were here to see this.

The day turns hot with temperatures soaring to ninety degrees. Thankfully I have an energy drink mix to help me along the hottest part of the trail and when I'm feeling fatigued. My legs get fairly toasted before I remember to put on some sunscreen. An itchy heat rash is also materializing to add to the first aid picture of desert and swamp hiking. Blisters are popping out on my toes from the sudden shift from water to a heated, sandy trail. My limbs are starting to disintegrate.

Finally I come to the end of my seventeen-mile wander to see the car and Papa's outstretched hand holding a bottle of cold lemonade. When I tell him about the wildlife I've seen, he shares his own gator stories, having seen several sauntering across the highway while being shuttled down to the Oasis Visitor Center. He also shares a surprise for the evening—a place to stay in a nice hotel suite in Clewiston. It's a perfect refuge to get rid of tons of mud and swamp things and rest. "We deserve it," he says. "We are celebrating surviving the swamp."

I can't help but agree. I'm ready to ditch my swamp shoes for a good pair with new insoles. I can't wait to clean up and launder our muddy clothes. More importantly, despite the issues with schedules and the brutal hiking so far, we are on schedule for the beachside cottage Christmas Eve. So long as nothing else sneaks in to disrupt it all.

But this is the Florida Trail. Anything can happen.

CHAPTER FIVE

BLOODSUCKING ALLEY

THE CANAL WALK

Our stay in the palatial hotel suite ends far too quickly, and soon we are returning to the trail that runs through the heart of the Seminole Indian Reservation. Papa Bliss is also feeling better, so I won't have to tackle the canal route alone. We had talked about the possibility if he was still having the groin pain, but thankfully he's okay to hike. I rest at a small outdoor café, sipping on a large lemonade and repacking food while Papa parks the car at the campground after we obtain permission to leave it there for two weeks. While I wait, I watch a little girl blissfully staring at a Christmas cartoon on television, and suddenly it dawns on me that the holiday is just around the corner. It sure doesn't feel like it. While we never have much of a white Christmas living in Virginia, we still experience cold weather by seeing our breath in foggy clouds of air and enjoying frosty mornings. Here in Florida it's shorts and T-shirt weather, looking at palm trees in the bright sunshine, experiencing sunburn and heat rash. But there is evidence of the season in a few lights strung up along a fence and some cheery inflatables parked on front lawns. Yes, it is the Christmas season, even though it might as well be Christmas in July by Florida standards.

Papa Bliss walks back from the RV park, and we head out for a long roadwalk through the center of town. The sun is piercing and hot. Out come the sunglasses and sunscreen. At the far end of town, a convenience store provides a nice respite with ice cream and air conditioning before we hit the road again.

From now until we reach Lake Okeechobee, we will be hiking along levees bordering a canal system, constructed as a means of irrigating vast sugarcane fields and managing the high water table at sea level. While the hiking is flat, there is no shade to speak of, and this concerns Papa Bliss. He can sweat buckets even when temperatures hover at the freezing mark. Thankfully a few clouds drift by to hide the blazing sun. But when the red ball of fire does appear, we must find shade wherever we can—even if it's shadows created by the guardrails at road intersections. One has to get creative out here for safety's sake and to prevent heat-related issues.

The trail pivots away from the main road, and we approach our first water cache of this section. Before the hike we planted a series of plastic gallon water jugs in this section of trail. The nearby canal water contains agricultural runoff, not to mention gators taking long soaks or flipping around in the water. Once we reach the cache, we figure we have about another mile to walk before we need to look for camping. Papa instructs me on where to find the two bottles he placed in the brush, just beyond a large water structure building.

I meander down the hillside to find an empty jug and the other jug with teeth marks in it and only half full. "Oh no, it's been disturbed!" I call back to him. I fear what will happen if the same fate has befallen the other caches. All that work to plant the drops, even causing us to run late that first day in the Big Cypress swamp, and our drops have been mauled by wild creatures. What animals actually live out here, I have no idea. Unless a gator found a plastic bottle tempting, like he doesn't get enough water in a canal. But right now we do not have enough water between us to make it through the night and into the next day before we reach our next cache.

Papa Bliss gazes at the normally unmanned building behind us and a truck parked beside it. "I'm going to see if anyone is around," he declares.

I follow him to the gate where we find two people wearing uniforms of the National Geological Survey, just wrapping up for the day. Papa shares with a young woman the sad tale of some ferocious animal wreaking havoc upon two unsuspecting hikers by drinking their water.

"I've got some distilled water in the back of the truck here," she says. "How much do you need?"

We take a gallon and thank her profusely. Returning to the trail, Papa Bliss shakes his head. "I can't believe this. First our water cache is disturbed. Then there just happens to be someone on duty at the building who has water in the back of her truck!" I listen to him marvel, like a young kid given a gift when he least expects it. I should likewise be amazed. But I've seen God provide in many instances on my hikes and always when I need it. I can recall walking a lone trail in drought conditions and finding some unnamed water source that wasn't on my map. I've even seen water spurt out of a hillside. One time on the Appalachian Trail in Vermont, there was no water except beaver ponds, and the temperatures soared into the eighties. I got so dehydrated, I thought I would faint. I arrived at the lean-to to find a woman pumping water out of a stream, and she gave me all the treated water I needed. Yes, God's provision through others is amazing.

We walk down the gravel roadway atop a levee with

canals on both sides and sugarcane fields beyond. The sun is sinking low in the sky. We finally decide to set up alongside the gravel road, praying our tents aren't run over by some official driving down the levee at night. Our trail guide warns hikers *not* to camp on the levee, but there isn't much choice.

I try to pound tent stakes into solid ground using a chunk of limestone, only to have the stone disintegrate after several attempts. Papa Bliss finds a tougher rock to do the job so our tents stand upright in the limestone bed. With sandwiches we bought at our store stop, we settle down to eat a quick dinner, watching the orange ball of the sun finally sink, igniting the sky in fiery splendor. I take a few pictures, enjoying the pleasant evening. A few mosquitoes fly about, looking to take a bite. And then a few more. I swat them away and continue enjoying the sunset.

Suddenly a strange noise erupts from the canals on either side of us. The next moment we're under attack by a cloud of kamikaze mosquitoes in full battle array!

"Quick, get into your tent!" I yell to Papa. We hurriedly pack up our stuff and dive into the tents as mosquitoes zoom in with us. I kill at least thirty that made it in before I could zip up the tent door. They cling to the netting, hundreds of them, hungrily gazing at me, so desiring a snack. The unending buzzing outside my dwelling is maddening.

And then I make a most unpleasant discovery. I haven't done my business, forgetting all about it in the hustle and bustle of outrunning a determined enemy. It's tough being a woman out here with all we have to do, from the bathroom issue to dealing with periods, the lack of muscular strength for certain activities, to the gift of intuition that no guy believes is correct unless he sees it for himself. Now I have to venture out into mosquito hell, where the insects are licking their lips and readying their long spikes or whatever it is that lances the skin. I throw on my rain gear and my head net and dash out to do my business, praying the insects don't bite unmentionable places.

The buzzing endures all night. I inform Papa we're going to have to delay our departure until the skeeters retreat to the wetlands around the canals. The thought of trying to fight off biting madness while dismantling the campsite goes beyond common sense. When the first rays of morning sun appear, the insects begin their slow retreat, and finally the coast is clear for us to pack up and hike on. What a crazy night.

So far canal walking is not turning out to be a hiker picnic. What may be flat in elevation and terrain does not compare to the other obstacles one faces, like ruptured water caches, hungry mosquitoes, and rocky ground on tender feet. And here I thought the swamp was bad...

Today at least is cool and overcast, much to Papa's delight. His initial fear in this section is not intact water caches but hot temperatures with no shade and the ordeal of sweating for miles. We arrive at the next station—and another large water structure. The trail in this section goes by many water control structures that watch over the canal system like dutiful guards. Presumably they are there for issues like hurricanes that can quickly inundate the near-zero elevation area and for managing the water situation as needed.

Not far from the building is a pleasant picnic shelter and home to our second water cache. I'm a tad nervous, wondering if this drop has likewise been compromised. But I emerge from the scrub brush with two intact gallons of water, and we promptly decide to cook dinner right there rather than carry out large amounts of water for the night. With the overcast skies and slight wind, I become chilled and have to don my rain jacket. Papa sings praises that the hot sun is being kept at bay. Little blessings mean the most, as I find out many times when my feet hit the trail. All the things one takes for granted in basic necessities, like having good water to drink and the sweet covering of clouds to keep us from heat exhaustion and using up our water too quickly, are all heaven-sent to a weary hiker.

The trail now spills out onto a roadway opposite a tall dike. Overhead, a plane makes loop de loops as the pilot attempts to learn different flying techniques. Two planes then appear, one a biplane, and they entertain us for most of the afternoon. Along this stretch we catch glimpses of civilization in a few homes near the road. I think of these people living out in the middle of nowhere, far from the typical scenes Florida is known for—the beaches, the tourist attractions, the shopping meccas. For a moment I nearly pinch myself to remind me that this *is* Florida I'm walking through and not a state somewhere in the Midwest.

Suddenly I feel something pinching my leg. I look down to find that tiny pointed burrs have hitchhiked onto my socks. I pull it off to find the things attached by sharp little spikes. I pull off another, then another, trying to avoid getting lanced by the spikes. My socks are covered in these pointy, nasty things called sandspurs that pierce material and poke my skin. As we enter a field to camp for the night, I think what those things could do to my sleeping pad if I lay on top of them! How easy it would be to have a punctured pad and my trip ruined. I do a painstaking search of the ground before I set up my tent. I also check over my clothes and backpack to make sure I don't carry sandspurs into the tent with me. It's just another unexpected hazard discovered on the trail.

And speaking of hazards this evening, I must keep a careful eye on my timepiece. At approximately 5:45 P.M. the bugle sounds for the enemy to fly in for a bombing run. Right on schedule the mosquitoes rise up out of the canal with a maddening buzz. But we are now wise to their ways and enter our tents before the attack begins. Papa Bliss does a minute by minute count of the enemy hanging out on the netting to his tent—ten, twenty, fifty, a hundred and more, all of them disappointed in missing out on the blood cell feast. I'm just happy they don't seem as numerous as the previous night, and maybe my nightly trip for when nature calls won't be a race against the bite.

When I do venture out in the middle of the night, the air is crisp and the mosquitoes have vanished. Millions of stars paint a portrait of beauty rarely seen back home. I see constellations I never knew existed. This is flat land, with no visible light pollution from humankind or even the light of the moon, nor any groves of trees blocking the night sky. This is an astronomer's delight. Papa is up too, and we talk some. We cuddle in his tiny tent on a one man air mattress. I pray all the time there are no burrs under the pad, and most of all, that it doesn't burst with our combined weight. It's a unique night there on the trail in a lone field under a drape of fine stars.

A clear blue sky greets us in the morning, and I slather on the sunscreen even as my arms and legs are taking on that extra crispy look of a sun worshipper from the days spent out here. Sunglasses and hats are a must. We cherish the water cache waiting for us at the next roadside park. We drink our fill while I air out my toes, until I let my feet dangle on the ground and suddenly I feel something stinging. It's a fire ant invasion! I've never dealt with fire ants on home turf. The ants of Virginia are cool and collected and only looking for food for their colony. These guys are miniature monsters, ready to bite an unsuspecting victim. Yet another lesson learned out here—watch where you put your bare feet.

At the roadside picnic table, I place a call to my son who once shared in an adventure with me some years ago as we hiked the Appalachian Trail together.[6] I wish in some ways he was here with us, but he has his own life now, though I nurse fond memories of the journey we shared together. The holidays always bring out a desire to be with loved ones. Here in Florida, on some lowly canal, it's hard to believe Christmas is just around the corner. But the holiday spirit is alive and in full swing when a pickup truck stops as we're taking our rest. A friendly farmer stares at us as if trying to believe we are out here backpacking these roads and levees and asks if we need a ride to town for supplies. We don't, but we appreciate his kindness.

Papa Bliss now points out his next irritation with the Florida Trail, among several he's had. The trail is set to head over a series of levees in a six-mile square, eventually intersecting the same road we are on now, but a few miles away. He asks why the trail doesn't just go up the road. I can hear it in his voice—he's perfectly satisfied taking the shortcut to intersect the trail. I try convincing him to do the square dance with visions of palm trees and other interesting things. Plus the fact I have no interest in skipping parts of the trail. He reluctantly decides to tag along rather than be left behind.

It's hot on this shadeless portion of the levee walk, making us yearn for the cloud cover we enjoyed in days past. We head for twin dots on the horizon—the only palm trees found along this stretch of trail and our visionary goal for our next rest stop. As they grow bigger with each step, we trek past fields upon fields of sugarcane in various stages of growth. I had no idea our country even grew sugarcane as a crop until I came here. When the plants bear flowers, the crop is then burned and the cane harvested. Dark clouds of smoke on the horizon are from

---

[6] *Mountains, Madness, & Miracles: 4,000 Miles Along the Appalachian Trail* chronicles our journey as mom and son on this most famous long-distance trail and the lessons we learned about God and ourselves.

burning sugarcane fields. Yesterday as we walked, the air teemed with a strange, sweet smell of burning cane and carried clouds of ash with it. I noticed the black ash on my arms and legs. The trail guide warns hikers to avoid camping near any flowering sugarcane as harvesters can burn the fields night and day. It's all interesting and unique.

We arrive at the twin palm trees for some much-needed rest and the only shade in this canal wasteland. I notice the nasty sandspurs littering the ground, and since I don't want my treasured seat pad punctured, I carefully clear the ground to enjoy the bit of shade generated by the palms at high noon. We share a snack, drink water, and say little to conserve energy.

Along the afternoon jaunt, we make the ninety-degree turns in the square configuration, headed for the same road from whence we started, amid Papa's grumbles. It takes the rest of the day to accomplish it, and after we cross the road, we approach our final water cache of this section. Though the caches were a trial to plant, except for the first one, they have worked out perfectly. I can only commend Papa Bliss on his planning so we didn't have to rely on polluted, gator infested water out of the canal.

With the final cache intact, we scout the levee for a decent camping spot. Two miles away begins a stated no camping zone, so after about a half mile, we find some clear ground surrounded by sagebrush and weeds and decide this will have to do. Unfortunately the spot is right beside a field of flowering sugarcane. I envision trucks coming up in the middle of the night and setting the field ablaze right behind our tents. Or a truck barreling down the levee itself and running us over, even though the levee appears not to have been driven on in months. Neither are good scenarios of safety in my mind as I clear away the troublesome sandspurs and pitch my tent.

Afterward I look around the area and, to my delight,

discover a huge chunk of limestone with fossils buried within. Papa Bliss is a connoisseur of fossils. His love for them began from his days as a geology major at Colgate University. I've surprised him in the past with trilobites and other interesting specimens. Now I lug over the stone to his tent, thinking what a great Christmas surprise this will be. And I'm right. He looks it over carefully, identifying the specimens he finds, marveling at the remnants of ancient sea creatures forever embedded in the rock face as reminders of their existence. Dusk begins to fall, and we witness another awesome sunset, with Papa cradling his Christmas gift. It's a perfect place to spend our final night on the canal.

Suddenly a small truck stops on the roadway across the canal from where we have set up. A blinding searchlight snaps on and beams over our campsite. *Uh, oh.* Are they coming to burn the sugarcane field right behind us? Are they ready to drive down the levee and run us over in the middle of the night? Are we going to be fined for camping here?

The searchlight pans the area then disappears as quickly as it came. It rattles me, even as Papa takes it all in stride. An hour later the truck reappears to search us out once more. I half expect the guy to use a loudspeaker and ask if we are migrants or homeless folks. He says nothing and again disappears. The rest of the night we hear trucks roaring by on the distant road, hauling the same thing—loads upon loads of burnt sugarcane. I wonder where they are going down that lonely road. I wonder how they can do the same job of hauling sugarcane for eight hours. I wonder how they can stay awake all night. I wonder as I wander off to an uneasy sleep.

* . * . *

Today joy fills in the air. It's our final day of the canal

55

walk to complete another section of the trail. Again the sun blazes hot, but we have interesting sights to keep us going. Like an active train depot where we finally witness the destination of the sugarcane trucks that rumbled past our campsite all night. The trucks arrive at the depot, negotiate a steep ramp, and dump their load of burnt sugarcane into rail cars. I found it all fascinating—this sugarcane process—from the newly plowed fields, to the various stages of plant growth and now the final end at the depot, ready to be shipped out to factories and turned into sugar products. Most of all, I liked the aroma of burnt sweetness filling the air.

For the final miles to the village of Lake Harbor, Papa takes out his cell phone and revs up the Christmas music. We sing "O Come All Ye Faithful" and other Christmas carols as we trudge along the dusty road, heading to our next destination of Lake Okeechobee. The time goes by fast. There is something about belting out a carol that puts a lift in your step and joy in your heart, even if you aren't currently being inspired by a Christmas tree, lights, cookies, presents, or snow. It's nice to feel the joy of Christmas without the man-made expressions of the season. The joy that our Savior goes with us on this journey along the Florida Trail. And I believe we will see more of His hand on this walk as we enter into places unknown.

CHAPTER SIX

PEACE ON EARTH...BY WAY OF A TRAIL

LAKE OKEECHOBEE, EASTERN ROUTE

During the initial planning stages for the Florida Trail, I sought out the advice of knowledgeable hikers for tips on how to hike it. Two such hikers, Sandra and John, I met at the Gathering, and it's their guidebook I'm using to plan this journey. They give advice for hiking around the largest lake in Florida—Lake Okeechobee, otherwise known as Lake O. On the Florida Trail there is the western route and the eastern route that can be combined to encircle the entire lake, which occurs once a year in the annual Big O hike. For one hiking the Florida Trail, a hike in either direction to the city of Okeechobee meets the requirements for those hiking the entire trail. The problem is, many areas around the lake are under construction by the Corps of Engineers, necessitating trail closures that force hikers to take detours, often on dangerous, high-speed roads[7]. I try to keep abreast of the ever-changing closures, which can become a tangled web

---

[7] As of this writing, many sections of the trail around Lake Okeechobee are slowly reopening as projects are completed. Check floridahikes.com for the latest updates.

of planning. At one point I had decided on the western route that most hikers choose to do. Then I heard from a fellow hiker who had successfully completed the eastern part around Lake O. She puts in a convincing plug for it, with descriptions of nice lake views. I believe God sends all kinds of people to help with plans. Papa Bliss and I made the decision to hike the eastern route around the lake and also set up the lakeside rental for Christmas Day.

But there's a catch to hiking the eastern route around Lake Okeechobee. In several areas you are warned *not* to walk alone. I'm glad Papa Bliss has decided to do this portion of the trail with me. Although I've done several solo treks, I heed the advice, and he's with me in the dangerous areas of the Big Cypress Swamp and now as we approach Lake O. I'm soon to discover that having a burly, bearded bodyguard like Papa Bliss by my side is the right course of action.

Having completed the canal walk, we stop across from the Lake Harbor Post Office to rest and eat lunch. With the date being December 23, I post on Facebook my wish list for Christmas. It's not the normal one you might expect, like cool gear. It reminds me how most women like to buy shoes, but I love buying backpacking gear. I have two of everything, sometimes three or four. Like five sleeping bags, several tents and backpacks, and a lot of hiking clothes. I also love a good book about a trail I've yet to hike, of which there are a zillion, it seems. Or maybe nice lotion that smells like juniper (that would be a pleasant change from what I smell like right now). Even some earrings in the shape of critters.

My Christmas list today is the following:

A shower
A cold drink
FOOD

After hiking the trail nearly two weeks, food begins to take on new meaning. One starts thinking about food more and more as the miles accumulate. It becomes a major topic of discussion in evening circles. A hiker dreams of buffets. Sees visions of burgers. Hikers scan the trail guides to find the nearest convenience store where they can buy some good eats. Our plan today is to go to the South Bay RV Park, which welcomes hikers from the Florida Trail, even though it's primarily a place for RV campers. Most RV parks in Florida are for long-term residents who enjoy waiting out the winter season in the north with a cozy and warm spot in the south, holed up in their RV. These parks normally don't host tents, but on occasion some will open their doors to a nighty camper. But another bit of good news from my trail guide is that half a mile down from the RV park is a convenience store. I'm already envisioning what I will buy. A cold soda. Chips. A hotdog. A Christmas wish come true.

We arrive at the park dirty, smelly, and hungry. My feet hurt. They put us in a loop far away from any RVs, in a grassy field beside a canal filled with standing water. I immediately think of the mosquitoes bound to visit us this night. At least the bathhouse is close by to get a shower. But soon it becomes obvious, with the rush hour traffic zooming by on the road behind us, that to try and walk down to the convenience store and back would hurt our already aching feet, not to mention be a death trap with the high-speed traffic. I look at what's left in the food bag for tonight's dinner and find a lone packet of ramen noodles. Not a great substitute for all the food I'd planned to buy at the store. It's also Christmastime, and I'm not having candy, cookies, pizza—my family used to hit the pizza parlor every December 24 when I was a kid—Chex mix, or spiced apple cider. Instead I'm having ramen soup, and I make my displeasure known. Papa Bliss says he will try and go for the convenience store, but I tell him no. I don't want him turned into a pancake by a speeding semi just so he can bring me back a hot dog. It's so not worth it. Besides, tomorrow we will be in the town of Pahokee, where there is sure to be food. I can hold out one more day. I think.

We sit at the table, eating our ramen soup, looking at the Christmas decorations of one RVer, complete with holiday inflatables. Why do I feel like it should be July 4 and not Christmas? Maybe because the sun is shining, the temperatures are in the eighties, I'm dressed in shorts and a T-shirt, and we're backpacking the Florida Trail.

I endure a night with a street light glaring over my tent, using a headband to cover my eyes, and arise to face our first day walking the actual path that encircles Lake Okeechobee. We've already taken one detour past a construction site on the dike, but with this part open to hikers, it feels good to be on the trail and seeing views of the grand lake spread out before us. We share the paved walkway with walkers, bikers, and joggers, all wearing smiles and full of good cheer. It's Christmas Eve, after all, where joy and glad tidings abound.

Our only obstacle this day is walking through a planned construction zone, which we hear the foreman allows hikers to pass through *if* you notify them ahead of time. A detour of this section would involve four extra miles of roadwalking, so Papa made a call to the foreman while we were at the RV park, only to get their answering machine. Though we have not received a formal okay to hike through the site, we take a gamble the guy checked his messages and we go for it.

We approach the area with tall cranes and the outline of a brand new water station in the building stages. We look to our right, below the site, to see a mobile office with several trucks parked out front and men standing around looking at us. No one says anything, nor do they send out the flashing truck after us. So we proceed along the dirt road that encircles the construction area, praying we're still okay with this decision.

On the other side of the site a huge fence had been erected. To our dismay the gate is padlocked with no way to exit the area! We look to find the fencing runs down to the lake. Papa starts heading downhill while I'm moaning that we're stuck with no place to go except to retrace our steps back to that four-mile detour. To our relief the fenceline stops a few feet shy of the lake edge, with just enough room for two backpackers to scoot around and head back up the hill to the trail. Whew. I'm so glad that's over. Nothing like an adrenaline rush in trying to maneuver around a water plant obstacle course. Just when you think you've been through it all, there's another adventure waiting down the pike...or trail.

Walking swiftly along on the paved trail, we past a modest airport and runway, then houses begin materializing below the dike. Some are nice places, with fenced yards, pools, and lots of tall palm trees. At one home the family appears ready to host a Christmas Eve party, complete with a bounce house. Houses start to cluster together, and we now see a few homes materializing on the lake shore, including an aqua blue cottage with a red fireplug out front. I slow down and look at Papa. Didn't he once tell me our cottage rental is aqua-colored and near a red fireplug?

My heart thumps in glee. "That has to be it!" I exclaim. "We're here!"

"Already?" Papa stares in disbelief. We both hightail it off the dike and to the humble cottage with a screened-in porch, hoping we aren't stumbling onto someone's property. But under the rocking chair is the promised key. We've arrived at our tiny cottage for the Christmas holidays right on schedule. We gaze at Lake Okeechobee before us, only a few feet from the front door, with a lakeside breeze caressing our faces.

Inside the cottage is a tiny living room, a kitchen, and a master bedroom. On the counter is a note from the landlady, Mary, welcoming us with freshly picked vegetables in the refrigerator. Now I know I'm in Florida when there are garden fresh veggies in late December. A miniature six-inch Christmas tree decorates the dinette, along with a collection of ornaments in a whimsical white hen. On the doorknob is a felt Christmas decoration. We both hug each other in happiness, never feeling so welcome in our lives. What a picture-perfect place to spend Christmas!

After stripping off dirty hiking clothes and donning our extra camp clothes, we venture to the town of Pahokee in search of lunch and to purchase food for the holiday. We'd heard rumors of crime sprees in certain places, and this is an area noted by the guidebook where one should not venture alone. But being December 24th, the whole town of Pahokee is in the holiday mood. Music bangs away with townsfolk gathered on front porches and some older ladies behind large tables, trying to sell a few wares. Iron bars cover a few businesses windows, and I hear yelling in the distance. I'm glad for my beefy, bearded, honey/bouncer walking beside me as my right guard, even if this is still a holiday.

We end up at a seafood restaurant for lunch, where Papa indulges in fried conch and me, tilapia. Afterward we head to the grocery store to purchase holiday food. Before we came to town, Papa called our landlady to ask about places to buy food. She then offered to shuttle us so we didn't have to carry all our groceries back to the cottage. How wonderful to have a trail angel on Christmas Eve. The kindness of people is a gift we gladly accept.

We make our grocery purchases and wait with our huge box of food. A fancy white SUV pulls up. We chat with the landlady's daughter as she brings us back to the cottage. While putting away the groceries, thinking how relaxed I feel in our tiny home by the lake, I mention to Papa how nice it would be to spend an extra day here. We only planned on two days, but a third would make this feel like a true getaway. Perhaps we can also arrange for some kind of slackpacking venture to whittle away a few extra miles of the trail. Papa makes the call, and the landlady agrees to a third night for half price, as well as securing us rides for the section we need to hike. Christmas is here early. We are overjoyed.

The sun sets at the seaside Christmas cottage on Lake Okeechobee

*   *   *   *

Joy to the World, the Lord has come! We awake Christmas morning to find the sun rising over the cottage and setting Lake Okeechobee all aglow. We have no presents for each other, but we rejoice in the Lord's birth and all He has done for us. At first I felt sad I hadn't smuggled something in my pack for Papa to open this day. In fact it downright bothered me. When I confess I have no gift to give him for Christmas, he sighs in relief. "Good. I don't have anything for you, either." And we both laugh.

So today we exchange a Christmas kiss instead of presents. We cook a huge breakfast of omelets and cinnamon rolls and enjoy it on a small table on the porch overlooking the lake. We know that friends and family are delving into their presents, the paper flying, the oohs and aahs practically audible. Our presents are the soft sound of the gentle waves caressing the shore, the faint call of birds in the air, and the breezes drifting over us. I take time to scan social media on my cell phone and enjoy reading what others are opening around their family Christmas trees. Papa and I give video greetings online to friends and loved ones. For us, it's a perfectly meaningful holiday celebration.

The rest of the day we relax, watch old movies on the small television, and eat anything and everything. Suddenly we hear the patter of feet on our front porch. We glance out the window to find our neighbor, Julie, setting something carefully on the table and tiptoeing away. Papa and I exchange bewildered glances. After she leaves, we walk out to check. On the table is a sandwich bag filled with small shells, limestone fossils, and glass. Written on the bag is the following – *Christmas, Pahokee, Lake Okeechobee, FL.* We look at each other and smile at the wonderful present we've been given. The simple things of friendship, love, and a reminder of our lakeside visit warms our hearts and speaks louder than any present wrapped in colorful paper and decorated with a bow.

We want to thank our neighbors for thinking of us and look across the way to find them poking around their small shed. We head over to offer Christmas greetings and our thanks for the present before answering their questions about our hike. Suddenly the husband remarks, "Hey, we have something you might want in here. There's a red wagon we need to get rid of. Maybe you can use it to carry your stuff?"

I press my lips together to keep from giggling. Papa gently thanks him and explains we're carrying backpacks. We can't help but chuckle over the offer and realize that not everyone understands this trail thing we are attempting to do. But we appreciate the thought.

The holiday is topped off by a nice roast beef dinner with all the trimmings, and it's fair to say a good deal of my presents is the good food I've eaten. And then I recall the list I had created a few days ago, and high on it was *food*. Wow, I've gotten everything I asked for...and more!

On our final day at the lake, the landlady Mary shuttles us roughly five miles north on the trail so we can hike back to our cottage. The hike goes by quickly, walking on flat pavement lakeside, passing by large chunks of limestone with fossils for Papa to examine. We arrive back at the cottage to enjoy the lake and finish off the remainder of the holiday food. Soon it will be time to head back to the trail for good, but we will never forget Christmas in Pahokee.

* . * . *
.

Bright and early the next morning our neighbor Julie, the giver of our Christmas present of shells from Lake O, drives us to our starting point at Port Mayaca to finish off this section of the trail. Topics discussed en route include the dangerous parts of Pahokee that we were glad to have missed, and her interesting life by the lake. We exchange picture-taking and thanks before heading off to accomplish a decent mile day, if all goes as planned. Our destination is an RV park near Nubbin Slough,[8] but so

---

[8] A slough is a wetland, of which Florida has plenty ☺

far Papa has been unable to reach anyone by phone to confirm we can tent there. At least the trail here, which is not really a trail but a paved path, has excellent views extending westward across the lake. On the horizon one can spot various structures and towers many miles away. Distances here are easy to miscalculate when you think a tower looming on the horizon is fifteen minutes away, only to discover it's actually five miles away and takes hours to reach. Along the walk are covered benches, providing resting places for weary wanderers. Here we take off our backpacks, air out our hot feet, and enjoy a snack. I like having different points of interest to concentrate on during these seemingly endless stretches, like covered benches or towers or water structures. It helps make the day go faster, and I eagerly scan the map app on my phone for the next waypoint. I discover we have another water structure to cross, this time a working lock for boats coming in and out of the lake. And for the first time, it is *not* under construction!

Papa always hikes better in the morning, but by afternoon, as the temperatures soar, his pace slows and we take more frequent rest stops. At one of these stops by a covered bench, I see the lock ahead of me and decide to forge ahead while Papa lingers a bit longer. Reaching it, I hail the woman tender who operates the lock, assisting boats to access the lake, and ask if she has any water. I know Papa would love a drink when he arrives, and I'm plenty thirsty. I expect her to tell me where the hose is so I can fill up my bottles, and that would have been fine. Instead she disappears into the little building and returns with a cold bottle of water. I thank her and take a seat against the railing, waiting for Papa to appear while sipping the cold goodness that relieves my parched throat. He finally trudges in, his face and shirt wet with sweat, and gladly accepts the water I present while complaining about his aching back and sore feet. On a venture such as this, there are certain things that move and shake me while different things move and shake Papa. We have entirely different reactions to a day's wander. Papa is satisfied to be a camper, taking it easy with many rest stops, smelling the roses. I am goal-oriented, preferring to trek the miles and get the job done rather than linger in any once place.

Moving on, the pavement is getting hotter and harder on our tender feet. Papa tries once more to contact the RV park to see if we can throw up a tent somewhere, but no luck. We wonder then about the next campsite on the trail, Nubbin Slough Campsite, listed in our trail guide. We have already passed one such campsite nestled near some live oaks, with a nice bench and plenty of tenting. That would work, barring any issues with construction.

Unfortunately, as we close in on Nubbin Slough, fencing signals yet another trail closure. My heart sinks when I find the closed area includes the campsite we had hoped to access. Papa heads over to talk to one of the construction workers who agrees to allow us access to the campsite. *However*—and a pause always gives one concern—he can't guarantee the night foreman will let us stay or if we will be able to leave the next morning without being locked in. I refuse to take the gamble. Twilight begins to fall as we mull over our predicament. We need a place to stay before the mosquitoes start their nightly run. Finally I make the decision to backtrack down the trail and below the dike to a patch of long grass. Darkness is coming up fast, and I doubt anyone will chase us away under the final rays of the setting sun.

We barely have time to set up camp and make some macaroni and cheese for dinner before the bloodsuckers are out, forcing us to retreat into our tents. Neither of us are in good spirits as we had planned on different scenarios to end the day. But at least we're camped somewhere safe in our tents, knowing this is all part of the "blessed are the flexible" beatitude of hiking that I have witnessed many times. Before this journey is complete, there are bound to be more days and nights like this when best laid plans are exchanged for last-minute compromises and fixes. It's just spice to a hiker's life.

The sun is shining come morning, and we're happy to be heading into the town of Okeechobee for showers and food. Since the trail before us is closed, we must trek along a busy highway and walk against traffic speeding by at sixty miles an hour. It's a little over two miles before we gain access to the dike once more for the hike to the city of Okeechobee, and thankfully it goes by fast.

When we return to the dike, the lake views also return until we veer away for the last time toward the town of Okeechobee. I must say I'm glad to be done with this part of the Florida Trail. We have things to accomplish in town—the usual food, showers, and laundry. We also must rent a car to pick up our vehicle being stored at the RV park inside the Seminole Indian Reservation that we left behind ten days ago.

We have made it over two weeks so far on the Florida Trail. But now Papa must leave and head for home while I continue hiking another ten days. We make the most of town with food buffets, a movie in the theater, and for me, a short stint of slackpacking to ready myself mileage-wise before I head back out. But even with all the comforts of town, the trail calls, and with it, an adventure still in its infancy. Except now I am minus my hiking partner. It's a solo wander from here on....

CHAPTER SEVEN

Lost and Found

Kissimmee and Orlando

Sometimes it's wise *not* to read the newspaper. Much of the time the headlines blare all the bad news and none of the good and we find ourselves struggling for peace. Hence my inward dilemma just before I'm ready to embark on my solo hiking venture. Papa Bliss is getting ready to return home and head back to work. Just before he departs, I read the morning headline in the local newspaper that announces changes to the Kissimmee River. The engineers are planning to change the flow of the Kissimmee to its original pattern, necessitating the closure of certain river locks until this can be accomplished. Looking over my planned itinerary, there is one lock hikers must cross in the next section, Lock S-65A. If this is one of the locks the engineers plan to close on the day I arrive, I could be hopelessly marooned at the river's edge with no way out of the area.

I try placing calls to see if the lock will be operational around New Year's Day. The phones ring with no answer. Everyone appears to have gone home early for the holiday weekend. I look over my list of contacts and decide to have a fellow hiker shuttle me around the potential obstacle. I hate the idea, as that means missing a chunk of the trail, but I can't risk being stranded either, unless I can verify Lock S-65A will be open and a lock tender on duty.[9] There are enough adventures to be had on this trail.

Papa now heads for home, and I begin a three day anxiety-fest leading up to the New Year's crossing of Lock S-65A. I dub it my Lockness Monster days, with Lockness S-65A occupying my thoughts night and day. Especially as I try calling multiple times to find out its status, with no luck. These are the times when I question whether God is for this journey or against it. Especially when things don't seem to be working out. I begin this next part of my hike with a googly-eyed monster trying to disrupt my peace. Placing one's faith in the unknown can be nerve-racking. There is no sense of control, though I did try to gain some with setting up the shuttle as a back-up plan. But then I will have to return and hike the parts I miss. It's a no-win situation.

For now I try to concentrate on the trail and the orange blazes through the Yates Marsh area, but soon the blazes disappear from view. I try retracing my steps but find no trail or blazes after the double blaze painted on a tree. Taking out my cell phone to check the map app, I follow the semblance of a trail as best I can, including slogging through a wet slough and promptly getting wet feet. Eventually the blazes reappear, and I realize the phone map had taken me through an old section of trail. At least I'm back on track with the new trail but with wet shoes. On a whim I also try again to ascertain the status of Lockness S-65A. No luck.

The dawn of a new day arrives, and I'm determined to make it a good one, without any knowledge of what lies ahead. I camp near Micco Landing, once a nice area but

---

[9] Lock S-65A now has pedestrian gates that hikers can access, which alleviates the need to be there only when the tender is on duty.

now completely overgrown with a picnic shelter sorely in need of repair. Ahead in the woods I see freshly painted orange blazes, and my heart lifts. I'd heard rumors of a new section being planned to move the trail off the roadwalk to Starvation Slough, and it must be the new route has opened since my arrival back to the trail. How lovely not to be roadwalking for miles in the blazing sun.

Happy that I might be one of the first hikers to use the new trail, I head out. Soon I come upon palmetto fronds littering the trail. Then I come to a watery slough and my feet get soaked. After about a mile and a half, the blazes suddenly drop out of existence. The trail does too, turning into a mass of thick brush. It dawns on me that the trail relocation is actually *not* complete,[10] and an assortment of words I dare not mention here float through the wind. I only wish the trail had not been blazed, leading me to think otherwise, but it can't be helped.

I turn back, wondering if there might be an easier way to cut across land and hit the roadwalk and the original trail. As I attempt it, a hunter is sitting in a tree stand, sipping his morning coffee. I offer a sheepish hello, knowing he's not likely to see any deer with me standing there, and ask if I can get to the road from here.

He shakes his head. "It's all fenced in beyond where we are," he says, taking another swallow of coffee.

I have no choice but to trudge the two miles back through the wet slough—more wet feet—past where I camped last night, and to the road. What was to be a sixteen-mile hike will now be twenty. "Blessed are the flexible" once more.

I now begin the shadeless roadwalk by endless farmers' fields. The cattle stare at me as if I'm from Mars or take to their hooves and run wild as I stride by. Roadwalking

---

[10] The Florida Trail Association has since completed the Micco Landing reroute, avoiding the issues I now describe here and the roadwalk to Starvation Slough.

is part of the Florida Trail lifestyle, I soon learn. Out here, striding along warm pavement or slanted grassy shoulders, feeling the sun, seeing the highway trash, and watching occasional cars drift by, it's a different experience than what I'm used to on a trail. Of course the hiker also needs to take care of personal issues, for which there are no facilities to be found on many of these roadwalks. So I look for those dark shady spots, sometimes behind a palm tree or a small hill. I don't let inhibitions keep me from necessary duties. This is life in the fast lane for one who traverses roads. Out here you must go for it, literally.

When the roadwalk portion finally ends and I head for my camping destination, I suddenly realize as I set the tent up under the arms of an ancient oak that tonight is New Year's Eve. Opposite the fenceline from where I'm staying, several RV campers are celebrating the end of a year and the beginning of the next. When midnight hits, the campers set off firecrackers. I usually take time at the stroke of midnight every New Year's to reflect and pray and consider a few resolutions. But after walking in swamps, battling mosquitoes, getting lost, taking water from unusual sources while praying a gator doesn't come and bite my fingers off, I'm thinking my News Year's resolution will be this—to hike the Florida Trail and live to tell the tale.

January 1, New Year's Day, finds me entering Kissimmee Prairie Preserve State Park. It's already been an interesting start with a family of wild boars that includes mom, dad, and piglets who all take off running when I appear. I ford another area of deep water that comes past my knees because of missing a turnoff that skirts the area via boardwalks. Then it's onward through thick sandy roads to the park headquarters. I'm glad I made it, as the office is set to close in an hour. The helpful rangers supply me with detergent to do up my stinky laundry and soap for the shower. I then inquire about Lockness S-65A and if they have any information about it. Lo and behold, they know the lock tender there and even have the direct phone number. I nearly fall over when I hear this news. Even though the ranger tries calling to no avail, at least I have an actual phone number for Lockness S-65A itself and no longer need to play hide and seek among the various agencies.

I set up my tent on a small hillside opposite the restroom building and make friends with several folks hanging out there doing laundry or visiting. The restroom building at the state park is also the community area, not only with bathroom facilities, showers, and laundry, but tables and chairs, and racks of books, magazines, and games to borrow. I start with a bit of innocent yogiing[11] with the fellow campers, telling them how often I dream of something cold to drink while hiking. One lady then offers me a coke. When I explain the sparseness of meals as you can't carry lots of food in a backpack, another woman leaves and returns with homemade quiche. This is turning out to be a happy New Year after all!

I place one final call to the lock tender for Lockness S-65A and suddenly reach the tender herself! Yes... they will be open tomorrow—the day I plan to cross. Hallelujah! I promptly cancel my shuttle and curse the Lockness Monster that plagued me with worry for days. God had this all under control. Which I should realize, hiking as much as I do. But one quickly forgets such things when seized by the unknown, by doubt, by the lack of control, by trying to live by sight and not by faith. If only I have the faith of a tiny mustard seed. That's all it really takes for any monster of worry to move on and for me to experience peace. A lesson well-learned.

---

[11] *Yogiing* is a term hikers use to describe the art of having others give you things—such as food, a ride, a stay at their home, etc.—without you asking for it outright.

* . * . *

What joy, what bliss, what a wonderful time spent at the state park before I head for the infamous Lock S-65A. I pause by the Kissimmee River to enjoy lunch on the sandy shore and watch motor boats propel on by,[12] then head for the gate to the lock. I sound the horn according to the directions posted on the fence and wait for the lock tenders to greet me. They give me a cold bottle of water and a friendly escort across the river via a pedestrian bridge. Once I reach the opposite side, gazing back at the lock complex that once forced worry to abound, I realize all that worry and dread seems kind of foolish. Especially now that things are looking up, God is in control, my Lockness days are behind me, and I'm continuing north on the Florida Trail.

I arrive once more at a bend of the murky Kissimmee River, looking at the unappetizing water that is supposed to be my water source for camp that night. A man and his wife are packing up their truck at a nearby campsite. He's had a good weekend of killing wild boar, so he tells me, as the hunting season is wrapping up in certain parts of Florida. I tell him about my encounter with a family of wild boar upon entering the state park. He shakes his head and says it's good I wasn't attacked, as a mama boar is very protective of her piglets. I blink in surprise before mentioning my reason for being here at the river's edge, to fetch water.

He points to the murky river down below the bluff. "That stuff? You're kidding. Here, take whatever you want of our water. We don't need it." He points to a large water cooler sitting on the picnic table.

With happiness welling up inside, I fill containers with

---

[12] The trail route here has since changed due to a past hurricane that opened a new channel.

sparkling fresh water. I never thought potable water could make me so happy instead of an oil-slick river caused by folks in their boats. Water is something I can never take for granted on a trail. Between the water and a fresh orange they give me, I'm as happy as a lark and strike out with a jump in my step toward my campsite for the night. Even when I am awakened at two A.M. by two guys driving an ATV right into my campsite, with headlamps glaring into my tent and voices remarking, "Hey, there's someone camping here," I ignore it and go back to sleep. I'm too exhausted and too much at peace to worry about weird intruders in the middle of the night. I guess there is something to be said about casting out the monsters of life and being at rest. It works.

* . * . *

Next morning it's yippee-ki-yay, giddyap hiker girl as I head for Westgate River Ranch and my next resupply point. I pause at a caretaker's residence where I'm offered another bottle of cold water, my third round in three days. The caretaker gives advice on the upcoming roadwalk out of the ranch, including an offer to shuttle me along that portion of the trail. I politely decline, though the offer does make me wonder what's in store.

I hike on to the resort, and the first sight I see are massive teepee-like structures that folks can rent out (called glamping for the real beds, furniture, and other amenities provided). I know I've been transported into a place more akin to the image of Florida as a tourist destination rather than wilderness. The ranch is known for its rodeos, adventure excursions, lodgings, and restaurants, all the makings of true resort life. But for hikers it's a crucial stop to resupply food, do laundry, and have some semblance of comforts after many trail miles. I've not been in a bed in a while, and when I inquire about accommodations, the clerk quotes me a $200 price tag. The campsites are even $40 to set up a tent but they will give me a site for $25, and I should feel fortunate for that. I'm given a key to access the laundry room to do up laundry. There's places to take a shower and a small general store. But resort prices add up quickly when my burger and fries totals ten bucks. I have to purchase four loads of detergent at the general store to do up one load of wash. Ching, ching goes the cash. Sigh.

Returning to my lone campsite, which isn't that lonely sitting out in a field with three horses standing guard behind my campsite and campers opposite me, I repack my food and get ready for bed. The young kids in the opposite camp are whooping it up with music playing at full blast, way past hiker midnight (which for hikers is around nine P.M.). At ten P.M., and normally quiet hours anywhere in a public campground, I go over and ask if they can turn down the music. To my surprise, they do. I only have to contend with the headlights and buzzing motors of golf carts whizzing by all hours of the night—the principle mode of transportation in getting around this large resort. I wonder where these people could be going at midnight. With the noises, the prices, the sights, and the sounds, I must say the Florida wilderness is looking more and more appealing than anything civilization can provide. Trail life does have its advantages.

I'm up at the crack of dawn, even before the golf cart riders, and hasten out of Westgate River Ranch quicker than one can yell, "Giddyap, horse, make tracks!" I start out on a road, enter the woods, and end up walking along another dike. My only encounter this morning is with two high-strung cows ambling along the trail in front of me— and one of them must be suffering from bovine stomach flu. I know it because I look down to see a smear of yellow on my pants from brushing against the vegetation the cows have just rushed through. Ugh! Why oh why did the cows have to poop right on the trail where I'm walking? There's miles and miles of nice grassland to take a dump, and it has to be here. I use a baby wipe to try and take it off. So much for doing laundry with the expensive detergent yesterday at Westgate River Ranch. Sigh.

The trail guide now warns me that to exit the poop-filled dike, I may need to scale a gate. Oh, sure. When I arrive, all the while trying to figure out how in the world I will climb a gate wearing a full backpack, I see that the chain on the gate has enough slack for one lowly hiker plus a backpack to squeeze through. Whew.

The day can only get better, I'm sure. With determination I head out for a five-mile walk along SR (State Route) 60, a four-lane, high-speed, truck-infested roadway. I've walked a few roads already in mostly pleasant places, with low speed traffic and cows giving me the stare routine. This four-lane highway nightmare with trucks going 70 mph at best is crazy and downright dangerous. If one of these monster trucks hits me, surely I will be but human ooze on their windshield. Think of the opening scene in the original *Men in Black* movie and the large bug happily buzzing about, oblivious to danger, only to splat in yellow goo on the windshield of a truck. That could easily be me, human splatter on a semi's window, and the guy clearing it nonchalantly with his wipers while gunning it to his destination.

Not only is the traffic a nightmare, but so is the footing. The shoulder of the highway lies at a slant, and anyone hiking on it with a backpack for any amount of time is going to feel it. From this crazy angle I start getting hip pain. Halfway through, inhaling exhaust for over an hour, nursing hip pain, seeing all kinds of road debris cast aside on the highway, some of which is too awful to describe, I suddenly realize I *must* use the bathroom. Except there is no bathroom anywhere. I find one area to sneak away to, back by a locked gate and old road, out of sight of the traffic. But I don't realize until it's too late the bushes are full of pointy sandspurs. Only when I finish and hike out, I realize my pants are full of them, and they are poking me everywhere.

Dear Lord, help! This day is going from bad to worse. A wave of anguish is creeping up into my throat. Tears are glazing my eyes. I'm about ready to let loose and have a meltdown right there on SR 60. And I don't care if a semi plows into me.

Suddenly...I am saved by a grapefruit...

I lumber past a fruit processing plant with tears bubbling up in my eyes. But I brush away the frustration when I see grapefruit scattered all over the road, spilled out of the bed of a truck. I pick up a glorious yellow grapefruit and carry it the rest of the way to my stopping point for lunch, after leaving SR 60 for good. All my cares about a dangerous roadwalk and walking sideways on grass and the frustration of sandspurs in my britches takes flight under the tangy sweetness of a juicy grapefruit. I've survived being pooped on by cows, unscathed by not having to scale a gate, and lived the SR 60 truck derby. The worst is over.

Maybe. The trail into the Three Lakes Wildlife Management Area takes me along rutted sandy roads and into fields full of tall brush, of which navigation is a challenge. Entering a thick forest of palmettos, I lose the trail completely and must rely on the little arrow on my phone map app until I finally pick up the friendly orange blazes. If a day could be filled with challenges, this day is measuring up to be one of the more jam-packed ones. When at last I stumble into the Godwin Hammock Campsite for the night, I'm relieved the day is over.

The campsite is home to my first pitcher pump—a small pump-like unit installed for water. To get the contraption working, you first must prime the pump. Knowing this was coming up on my hike, and unsure exactly what "priming the pump" meant, I spent time watching a YouTube video on it. I asked in a hiker forum online what to do and never really got an answer. But on this pump are directions for priming. I pour a little water into the top of the pump and allow it to settle. I then work the handle, and presto, water begins to flow. I have nice water for the evening meal and save some for the next hiker to prime the pump. I then set up for a quiet night, eager for a good rest after a trying day.

As night begins to fall, another hiker trudges in. The caretaker a few days ago mentioned someone ahead of me on the trail. Now the hiker tells me he got turned around and ended up back here, so he decided to stay put. I think this a strange explanation and wonder how the guy is navigating out here. Does he have maps, a trail guide, a phone, a brain, or is he here for some nefarious purpose? It gets even stranger when he begins rattling assorted pans from his cookset at eleven P.M. and talking loudly to himself. Adding to this scene, a pack of wild coyotes are carrying on in the distance. Between the guy muttering and the coyotes howling, this is sounding more like the makings of a thriller flick coming to life. Except I have no intention of becoming a victim in said flick. I check to make sure the mace is within my reach, insert the earplugs, and meditate on Psalm 34:7: *"The angel of the LORD encamps around those who fear him, and he delivers them."* I hope God has dispatched a beefy-looking angel to stand guard outside my tent. One with crossed arms and a determined face to keep at bay the muttering, pan-slapping hiker lurking outside my flimsy tent.

As one can imagine, with all this going on, sleep is not to be my friend again this night. I'm awake early to pack up and sneak away just as quickly and quietly as I can. Thankfully the late night hiker slumbers on, and I quicken my steps through long grass, careful to observe the blazes on posts buried in the brush. Exhausted by two nights of fractured sleep, I wonder if this trail can get any more challenging. I recall my New Year's resolution—to live to tell the tale of the Florida Trail, and so far I'm still alive. But it's becoming more difficult to try and keep my wits about me and not surrender to fear and doubt.

Walking through the Three Lakes Wildlife Management Area, the Florida Trail comes to a major junction where the hiker can choose two routes around metro Orlando and its sprawling suburbs—the western corridor or the eastern route. For me it's a no-brainer, as I want more of the wilderness feel rather than going through towns and walking bike paths closer to metro Orlando. I choose to go east.

Arriving now at a quiet campsite at Three Lakes— complete with another wonderful pitcher pump, a picnic table, and a nice spot behind the palmettos to set up camp—it feels like a slice of heaven. The mumbling hiker is nowhere to be seen. I sleep like a log, and life is temporarily put back to normal.

I'm glad for one night of sweet bliss before the trail throws more adventure my way. I wish a quiet night wasn't so infrequent and the hiking day was more often without hiccups. Like today, as I promptly lose my way with incomplete blazing and no trail to be found. Even following the map on my phone app isn't helping. The trail is starting to feel more like a bushwhack through the primeval land of Africa. I look behind to see the faded orange blazes and realize perhaps the trail has been rerouted. How or where it is now, I have no idea. I do know the trail must end at a major road that leads to a nature preserve called Forever Florida. So I make plans to head for it, except the road I need to access is barred behind barbed wire fencing. I find a road paralleling the fence and, hoping for an opening to materialize, I follow it.

Big mistake. The road trace dead-ends in a veritable

jungle of cypress trees, blowdowns, and a muddy bog. It's like navigating the Amazon jungle, minus a machete and any sign of wild beasts like snakes and gators. The vegetation proves impenetrable, and it takes an hour to go half a mile. By the time I wiggle my way out of the tangle, my legs and feet covered in mud, I happen upon a cheerful orange blaze coming in from the opposite direction! Now the trail is telling me to turn around and go back after my hard-earned battle of the jungle. I wonder if it's really the trail heading north or another reroute that returns south. My map app on my phone says nothing, and I have no idea what to think.

Being a determined hiker who does not care to pay for real estate twice, I look for another way over to the elusive highway. (And I will tell you, if one is not determined in this world of traildom, likely they will not see the end of it.) Again the barbed wire fencing proves a formidable obstacle until I see a small area where the fencing is just high enough for me to squeeze under.

I shrug off the backpack, push it beneath razor wire, then crawl along the ground, reminiscent of a new recruit undergoing basic training to prepare for enemy encounters. Only my enemy today was that jungle that has robbed me of all strength, so much so that when I finally arrive at the Forever Florida visitor center, I can barely move.

I couldn't care less that visitors are staring at me as I plop down on a bench after obtaining my mail drop and spread my gear and food across a large table. Fatigue can do things to a person, like melt away any inhibitions. Especially as I had also been looking forward to buying food at the snack bar. But just as I arrived, a large party of eager adventurers comes in and swarms the snack bar. A lemonade is all I can muster, and I eat some leftover food out of my provisions, hoping the backpack will feel a bit lighter with some ounces stripped away.

I check my phone while at the visitor center, including the weather, and find a large frontal passage tomorrow plans to bring copious amounts of rain to the trail. I remembered a friend who contacted me before the hike began and offered me assistance whenever I came into the area. Now I unashamedly call to see if I can come in out of the rain tomorrow night. She agrees to pick me up when I reach the Deseret Section. Yes! When exhaustion sets in, and one is still frazzled after being lost and caught in a proverbial cypress jungle, the thought of time off the trail to collect one's wits and bask in a shower, a bed, and delightful company, rejuvenates the soul. I thank Dovetail and her mom for agreeing to take me in.

I enjoy the rest of the pristine beauty of Forever Florida, an ecological preserve and playground set aside for guests and campers, with wild grasslands and even turtles making their way through the mud. When one passes the roads with interesting names, including a road named after me—Laura's Way—it's bound to be a good sign for a hiker heading north on the Florida Trail.

The campsite I've chosen for tonight will have another great pitcher pump, and I'm glad as I only have a scant pint of water left. Arriving at the campsite, licking my parched lips, I find the pump handle lying on the ground and another part of the pitcher torn off. All of this signals one disturbing thing. There is no water.

Have you ever been set on something being there when you need it most and suddenly it's not? What follows is a wave of utter panic and the next question whirling about in your brain. *What am I going to do?* Obviously a pint of water is not going to last me the night. I whisk out my guidebook and discover there's a lake down a road, a little over half a mile away. I shrug on the backpack and make haste, hoping this will work out.

Arriving at the lake, I find someone has left an active camping scene, complete with a burning campfire, clothes tossed about, and a pile of you-know-what with toilet paper not far from the lake where I'm supposed to get water. Ugh! I double treat my water that night using a filter and a chemical and head back up the road. As twilight falls, I throw up the tent in a small turn-off beside the dirt road, hoping no one runs me over. All is fairly quiet, except for the mosquitoes with their high pitched whine. I just settle in for the night when the boys return to their camp, beeping their horn as the truck whizzes by my campsite. I worry a bit, realizing they know I'm there and wondering about the safety of it all. Especially if they've been imbibing alcohol. But then the rain begins falling and lasts a good chunk of the night. Not long after it starts, the truck roars back up the road, carrying the subdued boys who had bailed for the night. Hallelujah.

The all-day rain the following day leaves me fairly soaked but pleased that I'd made arrangements to get picked up for the night. I enter the Deseret roadwalk,[13] where it's approximately forty miles of pounding the pavement before I'll see actual woods again. And then suddenly, out of nowhere, Dovetail arrives! Throwing my wet backpack into the back of her SUV, she waits for me while I set out to hike the remaining five miles on the road, unhindered by wet gear. I swear I could take off flying like Wendy of *Peter Pan* fame without the backpack on me, as if the very act of leaving it behind has sprinkled me with fairy dust. I race down the road, light and airy like a wispy cloud. When I complete the miles in rapid fashion, Dovetail whisks me to her mom's home, just a few blocks away from the Atlantic Ocean at Satellite Beach. This area is known as the Space Coast—they have their share of experiencing take-offs from the Kennedy Space Center thirty miles north, with tremors that shake their house. The mere thought fascinates me, as does

---

[13] The Florida Trail Association is working to move the Florida Trail off this very lengthy roadwalk in the Deseret Section and onto public land.

the idea of strangers willing to take in a stinky, dirty, muddy, windblown, rain-soaked hiker into their clean surroundings. These trail angels go over and beyond the call of duty, letting me string up my wet tent, making me a lovely meal, allowing me to do up laundry and grab a shower. I'm grateful for it all and for the new friendships I've made.

Dovetail joins me for an overnight trip to a camping area off the Florida Trail the following night. Then I'm back to soloing it, walking the remainder of the forty-mile roadwalk along a four-lane divided highway until I reach some real wilderness in the Tosohatchee Wildlife Management Area. This place is my favorite area thus far, with lush palmettos and palms rising to the crystal blue skies above. The trail here is well marked, with good signage and plenty of Florida National Scenic Trail signs. I hike to the outskirts of a town called Christmas where the post office is said to get inundated with mail around the holidays so people can obtain the revered postmark on their holiday cards. Schoolchildren, waiting for the bus, point and comment on the backpacker strolling on by. I'm enjoying some pleasant hiking days now and finally having fun too, hiking through scenic places of the Chuluota Wilderness and views of the Econlockhatchee or Econ River.

But the time is drawing nigh when I must leave the trail and head home to deal with medical matters and a follow-up to the cataract surgery I had back in December. These final days are pleasant memories to fuel one's expectations for a swift return to the Florida Trail. Arriving in the town of Oviedo and the stopping point the day before my birthday, Dovetail arrives to pick me up and take me to her mom's for an overnight stay before my flight leaves the next morning. I spend birthday eve with my adopted mom—once a famous gymnastics instructor—as we gaze at the Atlantic Ocean and the waves caressing the shore.

It's all vastly different from what I've experienced these many weeks on the trail. When we return home, Dovetail and Mom light candles on a cake to celebrate my birthday. I feel at peace and grateful for everything, even through the tough stuff, on a trail that began weeks ago with Papa Bliss in the Big Cypress National Preserve and ends here just outside Orlando. Tomorrow I will wing my way back home to civilization.

But one thing is for certain. When a trail adventure becomes part of your life, and all you think about is that experience and when you will return, then it's bound to happen. You *will* come back to continue the journey.

CHAPTER EIGHT

IN SEARCH OF THOSE FINER THINGS

OCALA NATIONAL FOREST

You know a trail is in your blood after you've been away and wonder how soon you can return for more adventure. At first I had decided the four week stint on the Florida Trail is all I would do for the season. But in a matter of weeks after being home, I'm planning my return to the Sunshine State. I figure after completing various tasks on the home front, plus a myriad of doctor appointments, I'm free for another two weeks of adventuring before my summer job begins. I plan to start where I left off in January with the goal of reaching the halfway point of the trail somewhere around milepost 550 near the small community of Lake Butler. I'm excited to return so soon.

For a different start to the adventure, I decide to hop a train from Virginia to Florida. I'd taken train trips as a teenager, traveling from a rural station on the Hudson River in New York State, whistling my way to Grand Central Station in New York City and all the fun it entailed. Though this ride to Florida will be an overnight excursion, the cars have seats that recline. And since it's a reasonably cheap fair, I will arrive at Lake Mary, a suburb of Orlando, by midmorning with money to spare.

But nothing turns out the way I expect. The train's departure from Richmond is delayed by two hours. By the time I board, darkness is looming. A reclining seat that only goes back so far and with a broken footrest doesn't bode well for sleeping. Trainmates also bound for Florida—they assign you to cars depending on your final destination—decide on an all-night chit chat to pass the time. Needless to say, sleep is not to be my friend. Toilets in the train bathrooms overflow with a raw stench. It's like riding a train in a third world country. When I finally arrive, beleaguered, at the Sanford train depot and greeted by trail angel Trucker Bob who takes pictures of me (ugh) and drives me to Lake Mary, I squint at the bright sunshine and palm trees and try to tell my sleepy self that yes, Blissful, you are back in Florida.

Trucker Bob and I catch lunch, and then I'm off to the hotel to crash for the rest of the day. I did manage to explore Lake Mary later in the afternoon; a well-to-do community with plenty of shopping and every restaurant imaginable. I buy a new hiking shirt, get some food for dinner, and then head back to the hotel for a second crash so I'm ready to hike the next morning.

The Florida Trail in this section joins the Cross Seminole Trail, a pathway for cyclists and pedestrians, passing by affluent communities and over extravagant bridges that cross the major highways. The following day I arranged for a shuttle from Shelly, who takes me to my starting point at Oviedo where I ended a few weeks ago, to begin my journey anew. I stare at the Florida Trail sign at this junction, finding it hard to believe that I'm back on the trail for more adventure. I go but a scant half mile when I run into a fellow hiker, one I recognize from the Florida Trail hiking group on Facebook. This is always the intriguing part about hiking—you never know what will happen or who you will run into. We chat about the trail and hiking gear, take selfies, and then I'm on my way. The paved trail raises havoc with my feet, which are not used to pounding the pavement, but the miles pass quickly. In no time I arrive at my destination at Lake Mary where a healthy buffet lunch of salad at Jason's Deli is on the menu before returning to the hotel.

The following morning, carrying my full backpack, I return to the bridge where I left off yesterday to begin my northward trek toward Ocala National Forest, one of three national forests the trail visits. I never considered Florida to be a state that would have enough pristine woodlands to constitute a national forest designation. National forests to me are huge swaths of beautiful woods with camping and recreational opportunities. I look forward to seeing all that Florida has to offer by way of these national forests. But first I finish the Cross Seminole Trail segment in style, passing by some interesting and unique murals painted on fencing that borders the path, including whimsical portrayals of Winnie the Pooh, Smoky the Bear, and the Sesame Street characters. I stare at these intricate murals in fascination, having never encountered anything like that on the trail. It's unique, entertaining, and the artists are talented beyond compare.

Veering away from the bike path and completing a short stint through the Lower Wekiva Preserve State Park,[14] I enter the Seminole State Forest with the intention of camping that night near a spring. Just the thought of a spring in Florida seems a misnomer. There are no mountains in the state, of course. Water here normally comes from cypress domes, bogs, ponds, lakes, rivers, strands, sloughs, or pumps, and much of it tannic in color. I'm interested to see what constitutes a Florida

---

[14] The trail is now rerouted as a major parkway has taken out that portion of the woods in Wekiva, which goes to show how quickly things can change on a trail from year to year.

spring as I make my way past the first of several trailside shelters and then a few scenic views of the Blackwater River. The campsite I choose is not far from Shark Tooth Spring, named for the shark's teeth that can be found in the surrounding sand. I trek down the hill, and what to my wondering eyes should appear but water flowing out of the ground, clear and cold, and the best I've tasted by far on the trail. I collect several bottles full and drink to my heart's content. To top it off, I find two shark teeth fossils in the sandy bottom of the spring to bring home to Papa Bliss. What a great way to start my first evening back on the Florida Trail.

Of course, I assume after such a good start that things will probably go downhill. It's sad to say, but oftentimes a hike is akin to a rollercoaster of highs and lows in trail life. But I go forth into the new day, determined to accept whatever comes. The roadwalk today winds its way through a small housing development where a nice neighbor offers hikers her home to charge up their phones or fill water. I meander through some burned-out areas in the Seminole State Forest and then enter a sprawling Scout camp where I hope to find water coming out of spigot, according to my trusty trail guide. But first an orange tree with fruit ripe for the picking grabs my attention. I never thought I'd see an orange tree out in the wild like this. I'm eager to try some fruit, but one bite tells me it's not what I think. The fruit might as well be a lemon, colored orange as a teaser, it's so sour and unappetizing. So much for yummy fruit on a warm day.

Walking along, I encounter two women day hiking on the trail. The sight itself is an oddity. Despite the fact this is the Florida Trail, no one day hikes it, at least not from what I've seen. In fact I can count on one hand the number of hikers I've stumbled upon on the trail. So these day hikers are a pleasant surprise. We strike up a conversation. I tell them my plans for spending the night not far from the Clearwater Lake Trailhead, despite the lack of water in the area. When they offer to cache water for me at two different trail junctions in this fairly dry area, they become known as the Paisley angels. I'm most happy to accept their kindness of water drops. These acts of benevolence, termed trail magic and given by trail angels, are what helps make hiking such a unique and humbling experience. Folks I've never met go out of their way to care for a stranger's needs. It's a part of the trail experience that makes the journey special.

Energized by the encounter, I head off to hike a few more miles, happy to have the water situation taken care of for the night. At the road intersection, I come across a convertible, and sitting in the driver's seat is one of the Paisley angels. She says with a grin, "Well, I have some water in the trunk. I was going to leave it for you. Unless of course you'd rather come home with me and spend the night in a real bed?"

Did I just receive an invitation to stay at her house? I accept with great enthusiasm. She then produces another unexpected treat, a Häagen-Dazs ice cream bar. Can anyone say *double blessing*? Wow. Going by the name of Trail Talker, she chats about her life here in Florida and her own hiking adventures while silently I thank God for sending this kind woman to take me in. That evening Trail Talker and her husband treat me to a great barbecue dinner at a restaurant, then rise early the next morning to make me a cheese omelet. I am beyond grateful for their giving hearts to a lowly wanderer. Day Two of my return on the Florida Trail, and already I've been blessed beyond measure.

With a smile in my heart, I enter Ocala National Forest at the Clearwater Lake Trailhead, greeted by signage describing the Florida Trail's beginnings along with a huge National Scenic Trail sign. Soon though I exchange the pretty scenery of thick palmettos for a burned-out land and then desolation, with acres and acres stripped of all vegetation but for a few somber tree parts left to rot in the hot sun. The loggers have come through, and it's a most depressing sight. Between that and battling fatigue from the heat that grows by the hour, I'm not a happy hiker. But stumbling upon the second water cache left for me by the Paisley angels, my spirits are uplifted. I drink my fill, hoping the water will help my mood, and I take it easy for the remainder of the afternoon. Even though the trail is flat, there are times to pace oneself or face heat-related issues. Today is one of those days. That evening I cook my meal at a picnic table overlooking the pretty lake at Farles Prairie recreation area and then onward to a campsite amid the burned-out pine forest, trying not to turn everything I own charcoal black.

Unfortunately water sources on the trail continue to be an issue with the dry weather, despite having a great resource in my trail guide and the trail map app on my cell phone. Many times the sources listed are dried up, necessitating that I look for alternate sources. And so it is with a certain pond I find, surrounded by a shore of black soil, shared in Chapter One. That black ground soon becomes a black pit of despair where I sink up to my hips in deep mud. I fear turning into a permanent statue. Talk about a scary situation. Instead of giving up and returning to the safety of my backpack, I doggedly go forward. Again I sink down to my hip. Again I drag my leg out. Is it possible to be like Peter and walk on mud? I'm about to find out as I search for places where grass is growing in the black mud. I sink only a bit then as the grassy roots provide some stable ground. Finally I reach the pond to dip water into my bag. After filling it, I look for more grassy patches to return to the safety of my backpack, avoiding any further encounters with the sucking mud.

I look down at my legs covered in black ooze and can't

help but laugh, even taking a picture for posterity's sake. I'm learning the hard way about the muddy traps of Florida but learning that you can walk on mud if you're careful. Who would have thought?

Now I just want to release the pent-up anxiety and think on better things. Like a favorite classic as a child. I'm hiking by Pat's Island and the Yearling Trail where the book, *The Yearling,* is based on an old settlement there. I recall with fondness the movie starring Gregory Peck who played the father, Penny Baxter, with his wife Ora and son Jody, illustrating the lives of the settlers here and the trials they endured. I'm sure these settlers faced their version of a sucking mud moment. When one thinks of pioneers, it conjures up images of a journey westward across the prairies. Those who came to settle Florida forged an existence among the palms and palmettos and oaks, the mosquitoes and gators and snakes (in *The Yearling,* Penny gets bitten by a rattler), the tannic waters and swamps and tropical storms that are all part of life in this region of the United States. I wish now I wasn't hiking a high-mile day due to the sucking mud encounter so I could wander the Yearling Trail and investigate the old settlement ruins. Supposedly a hike is a journey not a destination, but many times I forget in my quest to accomplish the day's goal. And so I trek on.

Now I'm thinking about tonight's campsite and the water source located in a large sinkhole. The notes on my phone map app—where hikers can leave their personal revelations of the trail—gives dire warnings of a treacherous path down to the sinkhole to obtain the water. After today's debacle with the black goo, I'm not interested in any more issues and pray this water gathering at the big hole will not be a problem.

I arrive to find a huge sinkhole holding a body of greenish water. The steep steps leading down to the water appear intact, with only a bit of crumbling from wear and tear in the elements. I suppose when one does as many trails as I have, difficulty is par for the course. And I suppose by Florida standards, anything a bit steep or weathered-looking is a challenge. Though I believe neither warranted the danger posted on the trail app. But I'm happy to have plenty of water for the needed task of removing the black mud caked on from my feet to my hips. The extra bandana becomes a washcloth. I string up a clothesline to dry out gear. It's all starting to feel like home sweet home here in the Florida wilderness. I may yet become a tried and true Floridian settler, like the Baxter family of *The Yearling*.

* . * . *

The next section through Hopkins Prairie reveals why the Florida Trail is vastly different from any other woodland trail in the East. I venture through forests of gnarled oak, intertwined in such configurations that one might think I've been transported to a *Lord of the Rings* universe. The trail encircles vast acreages of prairie and sand pine scrub with trees standing as tall as multi-story buildings. If only I were a bird that could ascend to that needle-filled canopy, I would look out over a vast portion of Florida, perhaps all the way back to Orlando itself. In certain areas these tall trees stand alone, surrounded by acreage burned to maintain the trees' livelihood and prevent destructive wildfires. For a good chunk of my hike through the Ocala National Forest, I've struggled with the idea of prescribed burns that leave charcoal landscapes for miles. When I come across a sign that explains the reasoning behind the forest management of prescribed burning, I try to look on the bright side. The trees will be better for the burns, and the land will recover. Ocala National Forest is anything but a simple journey through woods but a complex cycle of preservation.

*A pine reaches to heaven, just one of the many
interesting sights near Hopkins Prairie*

I enjoy the walk among oak and pine before reaching
a side trail that takes me two miles to the town of Salt
Springs. Here I've planned a resupply and a stay in a
cottage for the night. The trail is well blazed, passing
by many wet and dry prairies and even woods where
prancing deer have survived the seasonal hunting.
Arriving at Bass Champions Lodge, I meet the friendly
proprietors who have my resupply box of food waiting for
me. The remainder of the afternoon I repack supplies and
wash out dirty socks and t-shirts, hanging them up to dry
in the warm sun. For dinner, the buffet at the restaurant
with old time favorites such as catfish, stewed tomatoes,

and fried chicken hits the spot for this hungry hiker. I like my stop at Salt Springs.

The next day's hike is through bone-dry pine forests until the 88 convenience store and a stop for a cold drink and some snacks. Inside the bar is already hopping at ten A.M. with older men drinking and ranking on people they have met in life. Only a small part of the establishment is actually a store. I hurry to purchase a bag of chips and lemonade and find a place outdoors to eat, hoping to get out of there posthaste. Just then a toothless man walks up and inquires if I'm hiking alone. Of course I deny it. With hefty angels and the Lord Himself watching over my every step, I never presume to walk alone. But the encounter warns me I need to exit stage left, and I do, hiking at a good clip to put myself as far away from the 88 store as possible. That's enough of a taste of civilization for this wanderer.

But I'm glad I did stop for a break, as finding water continues to be a challenge. I plan on filling up my water bottles at the national forest campground of Lake Delaney, a recreational area with paid campsites. Looking around for the tap or even a water pump, I find nothing. Two rangers see my consternation and immediately inform me that a water buffalo supplies the campground water. I'm glad they recognized my need and doubly glad I know what they are talking about from reading online hiking forums. A water buffalo is a big holding tank of untreated water for hikers and campers. After scouring the campground loops, I locate the tank off in a field and set to work treating enough water for my evening needs. While engaged in the chore, I watch fellow campers all around me, many of whom appear more at home on the Florida frontier than in modern civilization. I witness an older father teaching his adult son how to chop wood. A toothless man with a Pomeranian pup following him everywhere greets fellow campers, including myself.

Others are staked out in their makeshift campers that have seen better days, content to enjoy the swaying palm trees and palmettos on a fine, warm day. It's an interesting portrait of those lazy days gone by when my family once set up a tent camper in a campground like this. Now I've exchanged the car camping experience for a pack on my back and two feet propelling me along a trail in the wilderness. What interesting turns can happen along the path of life.

I wish now water buffalos were par for the course on the Florida Trail, or more of the glorious pitcher pumps I enjoyed earlier in the hike. The state is in a drought situation, making it tough on the hiker who relies on water to keep the show going. I've experienced little rain on my hike so far and none since arriving over a week ago. Pine needles snap under my feet. The air smells hot and dry. I wait until I reach the Buckman Lock over the St. John's River for my next chance at water. This lock crossing requires me to signal the tender from his little office across the canal where he then activates a switch to send a pedestrian bridge swinging my way. The tender greets me after the crossing, telling me about water availability at the picnic shelter along with the weather forecast. I stop at some picnic tables to fill a few bottles from the spigot, hoping the upcoming ponds listed in my trail guide are available for the rest of my camping needs.

The afternoon walk is a jog around a maze of logging roads, with ATVs zipping by or around corners, the drivers paying little attention to hikers walking the trail. To my dismay, the ponds listed in the trail guide are dry. The one place which still has some water left, several ATVs are buzzing through it, sending water and mud flying in the air. I look in dismay as my one and possibly only water source is turned into an oil-filled puddle. I trudge out to inquire of the ATVers now sitting by the mudhole if they know of any other sources. The one guy snaps open a cooler on the rear of his vehicle behind two small children and pulls out a beer to drink. He then gestures with his can of beer to the mudhole where they have just been four-wheeling, the water's surface shimmering with spilt oil.

"Guess that's it. Don't know of nothing else." He slugs down his beer.

I whirl about and hike out, fighting to control my emotions, not only for the ruined water supply but for the guy's idiocy to drink in front of me and the tiny kids he's supposedly driving around on his ATV. Calming the anger, I focus now on my current dilemma. *Okay, God, I'm needy once again. Like that's anything new. But You know what I need before I even ask. And I sure could use some water.* I sometimes wonder if the Almighty wearies with having to help Blissful the Hiker out of another jam. Though I know perfectly well the answer. He is not called Father for nothing. We have earthly fathers who help their kids time and time again. How much more will the God of the Universe helps us when we need it most?

I trudge on, crossing over an old railway trestle above a gulley, and look down to find a puddle of brown water below. Excitement streaks through me, even as the other part of me wonders if I dare trust the source. At least I can be sure, way down there, no ATV has been riding around in it for fun. Gingerly I walk down and scoop up milky brown water, pouring it carefully into my bag, thankful for at least a little liquid to get me through. I find a small place to pitch my tent between hills of planted pine trees, just off another ATV road, and pray for a quiet night and no drunken riders out joyriding while I eat my dinner cooked in brown water.

My wish for water is granted in full the next day in the Rice Creek Conservation Area, reintroducing me to the beautiful cypress trees and cypress knees I hadn't seen in abundance since before Orlando. Cypress trees usually mean water, and there's plenty of it. The boardwalks and bridges in the area are a work of art, showcasing the tender care provided by the trail maintainers. The area can easily flood, forcing hikers to sometimes wade, but because of the drought, the trail is dry. Even though water for drinking has been scarce, I can celebrate the lack of rain with toes wiggling in bone-dry footwear.

That night I enjoy a trailside shelter for the first time on my hike—Iron Bridge, an enclosed dwelling built for hikers by volunteers. It's a pleasant place, not far from a stream for water, and complete with a large picnic table. It reminds me of those pleasant evenings spent on the Appalachian Trail at one of many shelters, enjoying a peaceful night in rustic surroundings. While waiting for dinner to cook, I snack on a handful of sundried tomatoes. Many backpacking meals sorely lack in good vitamins that veggies provide, so eating sundried tomatoes has been my supplement of choice.

Suddenly...a chunk of tomato lodges in my throat. I'm in full-blown respiratory distress...yes, the hand grasping the neck kind of choking, alone, in the middle of nowhere on the Florida Trail. Visons flash through my mind of hikers finding me a week later, dead from suffocating on a sundried tomato. I'm glad I have some first aid knowledge. I reach down my throat with two fingers and claw out the two pieces of tomato lodged inside. I fling the stuff to the ground and gasp in both fear and relief. This has to be one of the scarier moments on the hike. Here I am in the wilderness with no one around for miles save God alone. No one would've known what happened if I'd taken my leave of this world at the Iron Bridge Shelter, a victim of a sundried tomato.

At least it appears I'm destined to survive yet another potentially life-robbing event, with which this kind of wilderness survival is making me uncomfortably familiar. Long ago I used to watch the show *Survivor* with men and women dressed in native wear, eking out an existence on rice and enduring multiple trials, all to win some money and prestige. I wonder if Hollywood producers realize how much long-distance hikers live day in and day out in survivor mode, wondering if they will make it through the next challenge thrust their way to win the prize of a journey well hiked.

Blissful almost met an untimely end at the Iron Bridge Shelter

Again that night, the *Survivor* reality show continues with a loud rustling sound beneath the shelter floor. I fumble for my headlamp and turn it on, trying to gather courage for whatever is lurking beneath the shelter. Is it a bear? A snake? A raccoon? An alligator? I shine the headlamp around to take a look.

I blink in surprise as an armadillo waddles out from under the shelter and scurries into the woods. The last time I saw such a thing was on television as a kid, watching *Mutual of Omaha's Wild Kingdom*. I can't help but laugh.

Yes, hiker from Virginia, this is Florida. You have made it through mud, drought, sundried tomatoes, and an armadillo. You are a survivor.

* . * . *

On the outskirts of a town called Keystone Heights, the trail veers to county roads where thankfully the traffic is limited but the sightings along a roadwalk are not. I've seen my share of garbage and assorted objects strewn about the road. Today I can add to the sightings a pair of Christmas socks, a flip-flop, and a full set of kids snorkeling gear. I walk by rundown shacks of homes and a fancy horse farm with a huge traffic signal flashing red to would-be cars entering its domain.

Today the clouds are rolling in, and rain is headed my way according to the weather on my phone. With speed I launch into Gold Head Branch State Park, grab some water at the recreation center on the way, and make a mad dash for the designated backpacker campsite that includes, to my delight, a huge covered pavilion. I erect my tent on the cement floor Rube Goldberg style, using large pieces of wood and stones to keep the tent upright, just before the skies open and a torrent of rain falls. Few words can express the joy of a hiker safe in a sheltered place during a bad storm. A potent cold front is making its way across the state, with temperatures set to nosedive into the thirties the next night. Florida is not immune to cold snaps, and hikers need to be prepared for changing conditions. The weather will not always remain summer-like, but a blast of winter isn't something I planned for in March either. While I should be prepared, for this short section of trail, I am not. This could get interesting.

I leave Gold Head Branch State Park under clear blue skies and enter Camp Blanding, one of two military bases the Florida Trail passes through. The trail skirts by some picturesque ponds complete with benches in an area that doesn't look at all like a military base. If not for the rapid gunfire I hear in the distance, I would have thought myself in some forgotten wilderness. But signs posted along the trail warn me not to stray while on base, and with the gunfire erupting in the distance, I obey.

Then I come upon an old campground site within the base and a dilapidated bathhouse from long ago. Once part of Magnolia Lake State Park, it closed back in the '70s, though some of the buildings still remain. The roof of the bathhouse has caved in; the toilet stalls are still there within a dark and dirty place that has plant life growing inside. In the rear of the building are the changing areas for the campers who once took a dip in the nearby lake. No doubt the base now uses this area for military exercises, but it was once a vibrant place for recreationists in a bygone era. It's fun to investigate, and I feel like I've stepped into a dystopian period, making for a wild, futuristic setting in the mind of this author. I'm also a fiction writer with over twenty-five books to my credit and always on the hunt for a new idea.[15]

After departing the base, I have one more night in this section of the Florida Trail before my time draws to a close. It's a good thing too with temperatures bottoming out, forcing me to wear every stitch of clothing I'm carrying in my pack. It's so cold, I can see my breath. Comforts and the trail experience rarely go hand in hand. There's always something challenging around the corner, be it weather or trail life...

...or today, walking the Palatka-Lake Butler path that runs along an old rail line. I encounter old railroad trestles in various stages of deterioration. The trail guide assures me these trestles have been reinforced by trail maintainers for hiker use, but we are also warned to make

---

[15] Find my books online or at your favorite retailer. My website: www. lauraleebliss.com

our own decision whether to use them or not. I come to my first trestle crossing to be greeted by a sign that reads, DANGER! BRIDGE CLOSED. UNSAFE FOR CROSSING. I look at the broken boards and gaping holes in the trestle and then the new planks nailed on top to reinforce it for pedestrian use. I wonder if the thing will hold as I look down at the twenty foot drop below. Here's to getting out of one's comfort zone and putting faith into action when we decide to cross the trestle, praying the boards hold us up. So too it's been a walk of faith on the Florida Trail, hoping and praying I won't fall headlong into some disaster like getting sucked in by mud, suffocated by sundried tomatoes, or injured by a fall off a trestle. Each step is a step of faith. Each step we take in life is likewise a faith-filled action.

I cross the trestle safely, only to find more awaiting me. The final trestle on the route is burned out, forcing me to leave the path and roadwalk around it. With this detour I pass a major benchmark on the trail—the halfway point. It's hard to believe I've come over 500 miles on the Florida Trail, but here I am.

At this point I leave the trail and call on a few trail angels, Janie and "Hammock Hanger," to help me as I prepare to return home. What a time it has been. Half the trail hiked, with detours, being lost and found, swamps and bogs, bugs, boars, and gators, cypress knees, an armadillo, palms, and trail angels galore. I've experienced quite a bit of adventure.

But...the second half of the Florida National Scenic Trail still awaits.

PART II

THE PANHANDLE

Halfway Point to Fort Pickens

CHAPTER NINE

IT ALMOST NEVER STARTS OUT GOOD...

OSCEOLA NATIONAL FOREST
AND THE SUWANNEE RIVER

*Way down upon the Suwannee River! Far, far away.
There's where my heart is ever, that's where the old folks
stay.*

I've been singing the state song of Florida in anticipation
of returning to the trail and the next section called the
Suwannee. Hence the folk song that fills my mind. I think
back to the times on the trail the previous year and all
that I learned. There's bound to be new adventures in
store this go-around. Thoughts to what might occur can
send fear raining down, sapping away the confidence
gathered in abundance from previous hiking adventures.
It helps that I have just come off a different adventure a
few months ago—hiking the Colorado Trail in the Rocky
Mountains from Durango to Denver.[16]

What a completely new experience. While the Florida
Trail hovers at elevations around 100 feet, in Colorado
I tackled 11,000 feet and more. The hike required a

---

[16] To read more about my Colorado Trail adventure, check out my journal
online at trailjournals.com under the name Blissful and Colorado Trail.

different type of planning and plenty of opportunities for God to intervene in miraculous ways.... Like my run-in one day on the Colorado Trail just north of Molas Pass. I always thought God paid closer attention and care on important prayers having to do with life and death. I never really considered He'd care about those little anxieties, like my anxiety over a maildrop box that had not yet arrived to its final destination. The box held the food and medicine I would need for seven days of hiking. That day, heading for Molas Pass, I'm hiking the best I can even though beset with worry over the box. Along the way I meet a fellow hiker coming from the opposite direction. The woman smiles and offers a simple, "God bless you." I pause then and ask outright if she wouldn't mind saying a prayer for this box situation of mine. She does so with gladness and afterward relays to me how this is the first time she has been able to hike in months. She's felt poorly for a long while and hasn't slept either. But last night she slept wonderfully and felt she had to take this hike today in God's glory. "And now I know why. So I could run into you."

I look at her in stunned surprise. Did God perform a healing miracle for this woman just so she could pray over my anxiety for an overdue resupply box? And to let me know that He cares enough about the little concerns to send people my way?

Miracles like this ready my faith for what's next on the path of life. And next on the list is hiking the second half of the Florida Trail. So I'm singing the Suwannee song and building up the excitement that I hope will see me through Florida's Panhandle to a glorious conclusion. I know so little about the Panhandle of Florida. Everything notable and wonderful about the state seems to exist in its midsection, from Jacksonville to Miami, to Orlando and west to Tampa. No one really knows or even cares about the Panhandle, it seems. But I care, as this is my next hiking destination.

I read about the Panhandle in the trail guide, with its many unknowns and infamous areas too, including numerous rivers, some even with rapids, the high point on the trail, the return of the swamp thing, a boat ride, walking through an active air force base, and hiking on a beach. I read how hikers in Bradwell Bay, the second most challenging part of the trail, must pack gear in waterproof bags for possible waist-deep water of the damaging kind.

Breathe easy, I tell myself, *and don't worry.* There is grace for today. Tomorrow has enough trouble of its own.

* . * . *

The time has come to return to Florida and start the hike rolling. I hop on a flight to Jacksonville, where I am picked up by Chief Duffy, a cheery man who served in the navy. Now he runs a shuttle company for hikers along the Appalachian Trail. We have plenty to talk about as he drives me to the home of a fellow writer of novels, Lynn and her pastor husband, Paul, who have graciously invited me to spend the night. Lynn and I go way back as fledgling authors who wrote dime romance novels (that didn't cost dimes) for the same publishing house. It's wonderful how this has worked out for us to meet after all these years. I remember her calling me on the phone when I was a new author twenty years ago and encouraging me. Now I'm here, ready to embark on the Florida Trail, allowing Lynn to witness the transformation of a novelist to a long-distance backpacker. I show her all my gear and my dream of a trail. I switch out my travel outfit to convertible pants and a hiking shirt. My books on writing change to a trail guide. I give up my suitcase for a backpack and ask her to find a needy individual who wouldn't mind having it. One can switch gears and apparel and attitude and life just like a mini superman. I'm ready to go. And right now, between the flawless flight and the lovely visit, everything is going like clockwork. I'm trying hard not to read into it. I've seen it happen too many times—all appears fine and then *wham*, you're beaten down by something. I've learned to calm myself by living for today and today only.

The day arrives, and it's a downright chilly morning to start the Florida Trail where I left off last year, a few miles shy of the town of Lake Butler. My merry trail angel, Janie, who helped me last year, now arrives at Lynn's doorstep to shuttle me to my starting point. I soon stand where I left ten months ago, staring down the long, paved Palatka-Lake Butler path before me. No words of wisdom fill my brain, just a firm grip on my hiking poles, an obligatory photo taken of me at the starting gate— courtesy of Janie—and then a deep sigh as I begin the journey, praying I will see the end.

* . * . *

Mistake number one comes calling on the first day of a new hike. I ought to know never to plan an eighteen-miler on day one. But it's not entirely my fault. There's no place to camp after leaving the humble town of Lake Butler, five miles from my starting point. I couldn't just call it a day after hiking only five miles, so I head out for the first of many roadwalks to the next designated campsite listed in my trail guide, thirteen miles further. In hindsight I could have shortened the day by finding a place to camp in the woods along the road. But I have no real practice in roadside camping. That will come later.

At mile thirteen of this marathon day, I enter a patch of woods off the road to rest. My right toe is hurting something fierce. I'm assuming it's a blister, which is no surprise. The path has been hard, and it's been awhile since I've hiked. I have some newfangled blister bandages just for this issue. Pulling off my shoe, I find a bloodstained sock. *Uh, oh.* Both big toes are sporting dreadful blood blisters, and one is oozing. I've never experienced this issue in all my miles of hiking. Yikes. Day one and I'm already reduced to a bloody pulp. I try not to push the panic button quite yet. Blisters are a part of soft feet syndrome. Walking on the hard surfaces of bike paths and roads and doing eighteen miles in one day is a recipe for injury, and my feet are the living proof.

I put on the new blister bandages and then ease on my socks and shoes. The toes are going to hurt for a while but should get better, I reason. I know too I'll soon leave the roads and enter calmer ground in the woods. Unfortunately when I do finally leave the roadwalk for the woods, the trail is flooded with water, left from an active tropical season that extended well into the fall. I had marked the area in my guidebook where water was noted by maintainers since the two hurricanes, hoping the areas might've had time to dry. That's not the case. As I plod through the water wearing my crocs, not wishing to get my brand new hiking shoes wet, the expensive blister bandages fall off. I can't reapply new ones for fear of losing them in the next puddle. What a dilemma.

Limping along, I make the final eighteenth mile just as the sun is sinking low in the horizon. Being January, twilight comes early. Darkness falls by six P.M., which leaves me forty-five minutes to collect water, pitch my tent, and cook something for dinner. I end up eating in the dark under the glow of my headlamp and solar inflatable lantern. Temperatures plummet, and I hurry to don my fleece. It's going to be a cold first night in Florida.

And cold it is. Twenty-eight degrees overnight. I'm glad I chose to take my fifteen degree sleeping bag for this trip. Who would've thought I'd need a winter bag in Florida? In the morning I crawl out of my tent to find it coated with frost. Sunlight glints off the frost-covered prairie grass. *This is still Florida*, I tell myself, even as I stand there shivering in a jacket and hat.

Today's destination is a fee campground called Ocean Pond, rumored to have one of the prettiest sunsets on the trail. I'm also in for another cold night. I find this out at a major road crossing when a motorcyclist makes a U-turn in the middle of a state highway to inform me of the weather forecast and that I'd better be careful (!). Arriving at the Ocean Pond Campground, I look around for the host to assign me a site. The host knows about the wintry blast again tonight and invites me to stay in their shed where he plugs in a heater to make it toasty warm. I'm thrilled by the tiny house that offers a cozy place to spend the night, topped off by a lovely sunset to make me feel right at home. If only I had future places like this to stay in, what with the cold snap appearing to hang on for dear life. Checking tomorrow's forecast on my phone, I decide it might be good to find a motel for the next night. My toes are continuing to give me trouble, with blisters on top of blisters, and a shower to clean off the areas might be a good idea. It's likely too I may have to cut back on mileage until the toes heal. I put out feelers on an online trail forum to see who might be around to shuttle me to a motel after my day of hiking is complete. And quite suddenly, I get invited to stay at a trail maintainer's home. Or rather an apartment belonging to maintainer Randy and his wife who rent it out as an Airbnb. I'm beyond grateful for their help and the offer of a hiker hideaway.

The next day I try to hike briskly to make the agreed-upon pick-up time at the road crossing. Entering the second national forest of the hike, Osceola National Forest, I pass the modest Osceola shelter built for Florida Trail hikers. It's a sweet little place, but I must admit, I'm secretly looking forward to staying indoors tonight. The trail then weaves through a maze of oversized lakes of water that formed within the rugged jeep roads. I try to skirt the water issue to avoid getting my blister bandages wet. The process is tedious and sometimes maddening. Branches tear at my backpack and clothing as I sidestep along the tops of steep banks to avoid the water, both for my feet's sake and the cold air temperature. When at last I arrive at the designated place for the pick-up, Randy drives up shortly thereafter. I forget about the tough hike today as I'm transported to a quaint ranch home and introduced to my little apartment in a separate building that becomes my humble hideaway for two days. The place is a godsend, as is the tiny bottle of New Skin I discover in the bathroom cupboard. The stuff smells like nail polish but looks like a possible solution to my trail malady of blistered toes. I paint on a good coating while trying not to inhale the potent fumes. It dries to a thin, protective layer over the bubbling skin that surrounds both big toenails. That evening after dinner, I show Randy and his wife Melissa my blister woes. They look pretty nasty, and it's a good thing we're done with dinner. Sympathy abounds, as well as a few wriggled noses and raised eyebrows, but they offer to help buy more blister bandages as my supply is running low, and I thank them for their kindness.

I'm glad for the cozy apartment as it's downright cold again when I venture out to complete another ten miles of trail. Randy drops me off at the place where he picked me up, and I head out to complete the trail to his house. I never expected to see a thin coating of ice on a pond in Florida, but there it is in cold, hard fashion, right before my eyes. I also never expected to see another long-distance backpacker this far north on the trail when I run into a hiker who began down in Key West in December. He breezes on by me, doing a thirty-mile day. I ponder how slow I'm going, with just ten miles to reach Randy's house, and how thirty miles for me would be the march of death. Something like that is easy for the young, I gather.

I'm happy just being able to do what I do and still make some miles, however many they are that day. I especially thank God I still have feet and legs that walk, even if they are battered feet, and a back that can carry a backpack, and the energy to hike even if the going is difficult.

I enjoy the rest of the national forest through palmettos and pines and then hike along dirt roads, minus the lakes of yesterday, praise be. I then enter Randy's property that provides an alternate route for the Florida Trail, complete with an elaborate trailside shelter built by Randy. I mosey along through the woods and tall grass until I see the familiar sight of the workshop and Randy inside, building a table. I admire his ability to carve intricate designs and make furniture and even build a trailside shelter. Similarly, Melissa is creative with metals and fashions unique sculptures. Such artistry blows me away. I'm not one for creating anything with materials, or painting, or pencil drawing. I suppose one can say my artistry is in the written word. But observing what they do with metal and wood, and thinking back on the intricate murals painted along that fenceline north of Orlando on the Cross Seminole Trail, I've seen some nice Floridian artistry.

Randy and Melissa again whip me up a fantastic home-cooked meal that evening and present the blister bandages they bought on their shopping trip. They talk about the trail and the next section coming up—the famous Suwannee River. They describe how the trail will have some ascents and descents to it, making it rather challenging. It sounds good to me, as I miss the ups and downs of a trail. I'm deciding the Panhandle is about to become a far different experience than the first half of the Florida Trail.

* . * . *

With toes painted in New Skin and swathed in blister bandages and duct tape, and fresh from two nights of apartment living, I head out for my first look at the grand Suwannee River. The river itself is a rather unappetizing tannic or tea color, like most water sources in inland Florida. But unlike other rivers, this one has rapids. The trail skirts the edge as the river meanders below me. The day goes well, except for one minor area of trail where I accidentally hike in the wrong direction after a brief rest. It's happened to me before on trails when suddenly I pass a familiar sight and think to myself, *Hey, didn't I just see that?* So it is here, just shy of entering the town of White Springs, and I quickly turn around and retrace my steps for an extra mile of walking. Good thing I planned to go no further than town and head now for the quaint bed and breakfast where I've reserved a room. It's interesting how I've been on the trail nearly a week now and have only slept one night in my tent. But that's the way it's worked out, and I've been safe and warm on some cold nights. And after speaking to Papa Bliss by phone, I realize that it's not luck causing me to find all these warm places. He's been a prayerful soul on the home front too, thinking of my needs and praying for places to stay and people to help me out. What joy and peace is found, knowing that Papa Bliss is holding me and this hike up in his prayers.

The proprietor who runs the bed and breakfast, Judy, is a fascinating lady, manning the establishment singlehandedly along with caring for family members and whipping up meals on her ancient gas stove. After I check in, she mentions something about a chicken dinner, which I presume she is making for her family. The house smells divine, and hunger is gripping me hard. I run down to the town food truck that Randy and Melissa suggested, admiring along the way the town gazebo that Randy built, detailing more of his woodworking skills. The hamburger and fries from the food truck hit the spot, then it's chore time with laundry and errands. Afterward I relax on the front porch of the B&B, my feet up, enjoying the breezes. This is the life, and a most pleasant one too.

After a time Judy is calling, announcing that the baked chicken, of which I've been inhaling the aroma all afternoon, is ready. I had no idea I was considered family when she mentioned dinner. I'm glad I'm still hungry with my hiker appetite in full force. We talk about our work as authors while eating lots of baked chicken and mashed potatoes. I share about my life, and the conversation then turns to spiritual matters, like one's faith in God, or as Judy says, many gods. I've not felt much of an evangelistic drive while out on a trail, but if the door opens to talk about God, who am I to shut it? I happily share about my faith and what it means for me to walk with the Real God who gives me peace and a way to eternity when this life is over. I'm not sure what she thinks, but I know that

Way down upon the Suwannee River...

sharing this reality in my life fortifies my faith, and I pray it blesses her too.

The next morning, after a nice breakfast cooked by Judy, I'm ready to see more of the Suwannee River. Beaches white like snow meet my startled gaze. Limestone formations decorate the river's edge. Florida is rich in limestone deposits, which I've already seen in the abundance of fossilized rocks and limestone holes in my earlier wanders through southern Florida. The carvings of limestone make for interesting scenery in this section. Large oaks dripping with Spanish moss provide grand arches to hike under. The terrain has also suffered severe undercutting by floods during storms, forcing the trail to take steep dives down and across these gulleys and up to new bluffs. I do a good deal of the ascending and descending that Randy warned me about, but the trail is well marked and well maintained, making for a pleasant wander. I see now why the Suwannee section is a hiker favorite.

Houses then begin to materialize along the shoreline, all built on stilts in case of flooding. I haven't seen houses on stilts since my vacations at the Outer Banks of North Carolina, where they're needed because of the many tropical systems that pass by. These massive homes looming above me makes for an interesting spectacle. The trail then diverts to roadwalking for a time, as a few landowners are not keen about a hiking trail roaming past their homes.

On this roadwalk I run into my first major canine encounter of the trail. The trail guide warns of possible stray dogs roaming the roads, and I keep a close eye out. When this loose dog barks a greeting, I do what I think will work to maintain a calm atmosphere. I talk to the pup like a friend. The lonely dog promptly latches onto me like we're best buds and now trots after me, even as the trail leaves the road and heads into the woods. This is not something I planned, but I let it go. Surely the dog will tire of me and wander back home.

For the next seven miles, the dog and I play hide and seek among the bluffs flanking the Suwannee River. At one point when I think he's given up and gone home, I hear a distant bark and know he's still in the vicinity. And then I hear barking clear across the river on a patch of land opposite me. The dog looks over from his island, spies me, and then does a running leap into the river, doggy paddling all the way to my side of the shore. I'm amazed by his energy and also fear he might get nipped by an alligator. Twice more he swims the river before running off to investigate whatever it is that dogs find interesting in the woods. His antics make for great entertainment during the hike. But it also appears he has no interest in going home, and I'm getting concerned. I can't adopt a dog on my journey. Nor are there any towns nearby to call for assistance. What am I going to do?

I arrive at Holton Camp, a place for boaters and campers that includes enclosed screen cabins and a bathhouse. I'm hoping someone here can help me figure out what to do about this stray dog. When I walk into the camp, the dog collapses on the ground from his wild excursion and promptly falls asleep.

The campground host looks down at the dog-weary animal and shakes her head. "Oh Baxter, you did it again, didn't you?"

I look at her incredulously. "Baxter?"

"Oh yes. That's Baxter, and he's been known to follow hikers for miles."

I tell her how Baxter followed me for seven miles this day. She nods as if this is nothing new and takes out her cell phone to notify the owner that his dog has once again walked the trail to Holton Camp. I find it humorous, but I'm also relieved not to have the dog following me into camp for the night. Once that's settled and Baxter continues to slumber away in front of the host's camper, the friendly woman asks if I'm planning to spend the night. She says there's plenty of room, how nice it would be, I should really consider it, etc. It's plain to see she wants me to stay, but I've only hiked twelve miles and want to get in a few more before evening. Filling up my water bottles, I say good-bye to the host and the dozing Baxter and make my way back to the trail.

* . * . *

I'm feeling better in some ways. The blisters are healing. The muscles are getting stronger. I've lost a little of that Christmas weight. But now I'm in the throes of a full-blown cold, the first one I can recall on a major hike. It began as a tickle in my throat a few days ago and each day the throat issue has worsened. With the way the weather has swayed from cold to hot, it doesn't surprise me. Now with sniffles upon me this night in my tent, it's hard to breathe. I toss and turn, blowing my nose in an effort to help my breathing, hoping I don't freak out in my mummy bag and think I'm suffocating. If this weren't bad enough, my sleeping pad is going flat, requiring me to blow it up every two hours. Sickness and equipment failures are a bad combination on a hike. I get ahold of Papa Bliss on the cell phone to spell out my woes and ask him to mail my other sleeping pad to the next town.

The next morning I find I can't talk at all. For most solo hikers, having a voice doesn't much matter. Who's there to hear you anyway? But I like to converse with myself, and now I can't even hear myself speak! It's strange when you try to say something and only a whisper comes out. But despite being sick and having to frequently blow my nose, I manage another fifteen miles to a sheltered camping area. The place is listed as another Florida Trail shelter, but it's really just an open-air pavilion. The wind is too strong for me to properly erect my tent inside the structure, so I pitch it in the nearby grass. Then I sit on a bench overlooking the Suwannee and jot an entry in my journal. Examining the trail data for the next day, I note that the town of Madison is a little over twenty miles distant and mostly on roads. I wonder if I have it in me to hike a twenty-plus-mile day to make it to town, especially as the only camping available is out on the road if I didn't. I think on it before scurrying into my tent when rain begins to fall. I want to talk over the plans for a big mile day with Papa Bliss, but my laryngitis is so bad he can barely understand me. He doesn't offer much of an opinion one way or the other. For now I decide against it. I've not done such a long day in years, and that first eighteen-miler on day one nearly did me in. Especially as I'm fighting a cold, it's probably not a good idea. I sigh and snuggle in my bag, thankful I can breathe a bit better tonight. I leave the worry of tomorrow for the day when I turn from hiker to a veritable Road Runner—i.e... Roadwalker. Beep! Beep!

Just please, God, let there be no Wile E. Coyotes looking to get me!

CHAPTER TEN

WILE E. COYOTE VS. THE ROAD RUNNER

THE ROADWALK

On the Florida Trail, as well as other trails I have done like the Allegheny Trail, roadwalking is part of the hiking experience. While it's much more pleasant, and yes safer, to follow a trail in the woods or even over bare summits or rock scrambles, roadwalking lends itself to a different kind of trail time. Most hikers wouldn't give a roadwalk the time of day. It turns them off completely. Me? I'm getting used to it. It's a fact of life on the Florida Trail. During Part A of the hike, I had a tough time acclimating to the roadwalk. I was not used to semis speeding by at 65 mph, looking to make me insect scrap on their windshields. The sight of trash and the stench of things rotting in the hot sun nauseated me. The odor of exhaust, the buzz of traffic, the way hips and feet are tipping sideways on uneven surfaces leading to pain, all contributed to a less than pleasant experience.

But as one can become trail-hardened after walking many miles, one can also become road-hardened. I begin this section of trail knowing I have fifty miles of assorted roads to navigate before I will see the woods again. I will also be spending my first time camping on a roadwalk. It's just the way things are as the trail heads from the northern region of the Panhandle south toward the Gulf of Mexico and the St. Marks National Wildlife Refuge. It requires a different mindset and good planning for a safe journey. I will be the Road Runner speeding along this part of the Florida Trail.

Right now, though, I'm contending with a full-blown respiratory issue that began as a head cold and has since settled in my larynx or voicebox. It's day two of not being able to say anything. But looking at the mileage and the idea of spending a night on the road, which I don't care to do just yet, I decide to try for a big mile day into the town of Madison. The effort requires twenty-three miles of hiking, but most of it is on roads. In the quest I will be battling daylight. With darkness arriving by six P.M., I can't be found walking on the shoulder of a road. The nice thing about roadwalking is there are very few trail encumbrances that can slow you down. So if one wants to make miles in a shorter amount of time, it's doable. Which is why I decide to try for this hiker marathon. I had a good night's stay near a shelter area by the peaceful Suwannee River, despite the distant noise of cars rolling across a nearby bridge. I'm also hoping not to have any more strange issues along the roads...

...like yesterday's hike that included another canine run-in. This time it's Bruiser the stray dog wanting to hike with me. He was a big fellow too, hence the nickname, but older and kind-hearted. We walked together about a mile before we encountered a prison work crew, guarded by an officer and police van. Bruiser sensed the anxiety for the situation, it seemed, for he turned around and hightailed it for home, leaving me to contend with the armed officer and six prisoners in black and white pinstripe, performing garbage detail. One dude greeted me as I passed by. No one else spoke or even seemed to care, as if a backpacker walking along here was commonplace. I kept my gaze focused straight ahead and quickly moved on.

Then I saw smoke rising up in the distance, and I stopped short. As if there weren't enough things to watch out for in dogs and people, hikers must also contend with prescribed burning on the Florida Trail. For some reason the state conducts their forest burns right at the height of the hiker season, which in Florida runs from December through March. The telltale funnel of smoke in the distance means a burn is going on right about where I'm supposed to veer off the road and back into the woods. I wish there was a way to alert hikers to these pending issues. No one wants to be caught in a wildfire situation. Thankfully, when I reached the trail junction, the fire was located on the other side of the road from where I entered the woods. I followed the first sigh of relief with a close second, having endured in a matter of one hour a dog, a prisoner detail, and fires.

So with a bright sunshiny day ahead of me, my cold symptoms slightly better, my confidence fairly high, I'm ready to embark on this twenty-three-mile marathon to Madison. The first part is an enjoyable walk through pure Florida woodlands filled with scrub oak and palmettos to give the hike that tropical feel. At Mill Creek I hope to camel up on water for the upcoming roadwalk. Venturing down the path toward the river colored like tea, foamy and unappetizing, I happen to look to my left and find water bubbling out of a hillside, running clear and cold. I've stumbled upon a natural spring. Usually I end up with tannic, warm water from a bog or the river. This spring is an unexpected treat, and I relish it, along with eating snacks at the picnic table provided and tossing my trash in a big garbage barrel. What luxury by hiker standards.

Now begins the adventure of transitioning from hiker to the Roadwalker. Beep! Beep! I gear up mentally for what will become a fifty-mile, multi-day roadwalking event to include the rest stop in Madison. Road types, from what I can determine, vary greatly. Some are just passing farm lanes with no traffic. Others are composed of dirt or sand, many times without shade. Still others are paved roads that wander through neighborhoods like where I encountered Baxter the dog. The roads then empty onto main highways loaded with trucks and cars traveling at a high rate of speed. Drivers don't expect to see a backpacker lumbering along the shoulder. On my phone map app, destinations such as a church, a store, or some other interesting landmark provide rest stops along the way. At the end of this day though, I hope to be in Madison where Papa Bliss has reserved me a room for the next two nights. I use him on the home front to help make reservations and avoid the hassle on my part. It keeps him informed of my whereabouts and allows him to be a part of the adventure, even if he is not out hiking with me.

The day is warm but not insufferably hot. I stop at an electrical pole to sit in the shade, using the pole itself as a backrest. Shoes and socks come off to allow my feet to air out, and I notice more blisters popping out from this high-mile day. I'm hoping the extra zero day will help my toes overcome this next blister hump. It's been a week since they first appeared, and I'm ready for calluses to form and my feet to finally acclimate to walking.

I hear cars zooming along the interstate ahead and know I must be nearing Madison. The Florida Trail does a loop de loop with Interstate 10 that runs from Jacksonville across the Panhandle to Tallahassee and then on to Pensacola. Eventually the trail will dive southward on the roadwalk, leaving the interstate behind for good, but now I cross under the highway to access the businesses of Madison.

Congratulating my aching feet on a twenty-three-mile marathon well done, I traipse into a Wendy's restaurant, plop my backpack in a chair, and stride up to order food. I'm used to looks given by the public at the entrance of a dirty hiker and backpack which could spell the thought of a drifter or homeless person. Usually when I arrive in a town, I try to have mercy on the public and don a clean shirt—as I did before arriving here. But there are times one must cast aside inhibitions, even when ordering a burger and fries with my bad laryngitis. Just call me the Hiker Whisperer. But fast food never tasted so good, and so does sitting in a real chair after twenty-three punishing miles to get here.

Darkness has fallen though, and I still need to walk down the busy road to the hotel. I gear up to head out of Wendy's when I hear a voice calling out to me.

"Miss, hey, miss!" I turn to see a young gal wearing a Wendy's uniform. "You hiking by yourself?"

Whenever anyone asks me this question, I usually deny it. I'm never alone with God by my side. But it's fairly obvious no one is with me, so I simply tell her that I'm hiking the Florida Trail.

"Well hold on a minute." She rummages in her large handbag for about thirty seconds. I wonder what she's going to give me. Maybe a candy bar. That would be kind of neat. Instead she digs out of her massive bag a twenty dollar bill and hands it to me.

I stare at it incredulously. "That's so kind of you, but I don't need it."

"You sure?" she asks.

I nod, even as she goes on to tell me about other hikers she's seen walking the main road past her house. I thank her for her generous heart before she heads for her car after a long day at Wendy's. I think of the small pittance she makes at that job, yet her desire to give twenty dollars—the equivalent of several hours' salary—to help a hiker, speaks volumes. It reminded me of the generous guy in West Virginia while I was hiking the Allegheny

Trail, offering me money. Despite the bad news we hear so often these days, in the real world there are people working hard and giving from their hearts to help total strangers. They are like the poor widow in the Bible who gave everything she had, and whom Jesus, the Son of God, commended. I'm glad to see and share about these modern-day acts of kindness. I don't know the names of these trail angels, but God does. He sees their generous spirit, and it speaks to my spirit about generosity in money, in good works, and in a kind word that uplifts others.

Now I hurry down the road to the hotel for a much needed shower and a nice bed, praising God for the many things He is already showing me.

The next day is a zero day or a no hiking day where I do very little except rest, eat, wash clothes, hang out, and eat some more. I venture next door to Denny's for a huge breakfast that I'm barely able to order with my full-blown laryngitis. The waitress looks at me a little funny, but there isn't a thing I can do. I find also that my stomach is not accustomed to the fatty foods of town, and after several large meals, I'm holed up in the bathroom with a case of the runs. I think my stomach likes the hiker fare of rice, granola bars, raisins, and tortillas rather than fancy restaurant meals. Maybe that's why I adapt well to the trail life, except when I push the miles too much and the toes protest with blisters. I need to remind myself not to let hiker appetite get the better of me and gorge down rich food. Moderation is a good key.

That night Papa Bliss and I conduct our first FaceTime chat. It's interesting how technology has taken off the last few years, not just at home but on the trail. I now carry a phone that has a full map of the trail on it, serves as a camera, a link to the Internet and social media, has Messenger for anything people need to tell me, and gives the ability to see loved ones while talking to them via FaceTime. We have fun sharing about our lives, and time away from family is made easier with these modern conveniences. It's a far cry from the Appalachian Trail long ago, where more times than not I carried a dying phone with little reception. I didn't see my husband for up to six weeks at a time. But now that's changed, the good-byes are easier, and we say our farewells until next we meet by video chat.

Now a new set of adventures calls me once again. The following morning I pack up, equipped with my other sleeping pad that Papa Bliss mailed me and food to last me several days until my next town stop at the village of St. Marks. The weather in Florida remains cool, and I'm happy I have my winter sleeping bag and an insulated jacket. Bundled up, with my breath clouding the air, I return to the road for thirty-nine more road miles. Ready or not, here I go.

* . * . *

Can anyone say adventure and the unknown in one breath? That's what it feels like, heading out on a bright and sunny but cool day with a determination to tackle this road thing for all I'm worth. Roads in this stretch come at me in all shapes, manner, and sizes. The gravel roads are much better on the feet but warm in the sun, with clouds of dust sometimes greeting a hiker from a passing vehicle. There is the paved road, wandering through a remote area with little traffic, on which you can breeze on by so long as your feet hold out. Then there's the road with moderate, high speed traffic, necessitating that you walk on the shoulders. Fine if the shoulder is flat and grassy, not so fine if it's slanted or even nonexistent. Walking on any slope alters one's weight distribution, wreaking havoc on tender hips and knees that shout in protest. For these instances I do the switcheroo, that is, walk on pavement until I hear traffic barreling toward me, then take to the grassy shoulder. Sometimes the road will parallel a powerline easement, in which case you can walk along that. It's great for avoiding high speed traffic with all its noises and exhaust. Not so great if the vegetation is high, full of sandspurs or holes, or suddenly dives into a gulley or other deep ravine, requiring you to return to the road and cross over the area on a bridge. These are the kinds of things I face on a long roadwalk, and figuring out how to tackle each new challenge helps pass the time.

Roads can lead past interesting features like farms and livestock, where a herd of cattle are freaked out at the sight of a backpacker and start a stampede. The roads wander by humble homes, some nicely constructed with cheerful flowers and manicured lawns with sprinklers, others that are simple mobile homes or rough-hewed shacks complete with a variety of junk rusting in yards, chickens wandering about, and plenty of loose dogs— most of which are lonely and just want companionship, as I've found out.

Roads also go by churches, which offer friendly places of refuge to weary wanderers searching for water. I've already relied greatly on God's provision on this trek, and churches are a means by which hikers can refill water bottles and relax. Some churches even allow camping on the property. At the next Baptist church, I discover their lovely water spigot on the side of the building by some landscaping of fine stones. I sit down in the stones to fill my water bottle and relax. Afterward I see how I've disturbed the stones and painstakingly replace them so no one knows I've been there. It's a Leave No Trace practice, and we hikers need to be good stewards wherever we go. Tidying up any mess we create and carrying out trash, even the corners ripped off granola bar packages (otherwise known as micro trash), all helps in the effort. When I happen upon heaps of garbage tossed carelessly onto the side of the road, it's tough to see God's gentle creation trashed. He wants us to care about the world He made, like everything else we have been given. By being excellent stewards in all we do, we will reap the benefits.

Moving on, I look at my map app on my phone, trying to decide where to camp for the night. The trail guide does not specifically point out designated camping areas on the roads, as many areas are private property which must be respected. But the editor clearly writes about "forests" and "flat grassy areas" and descriptions that allude to places to safely pitch a tent. Some of these grassy places happen to be in old cemeteries, and one in particular seems to work out with my eighteen-mile day from Madison. A cemetery will serve as my final resting place for the night (pun intended).

I arrive some time later to large marbled burial plots of a bygone era and walk past these quiet places to the grass beyond, away from the road. This should do nicely for the night, but just as a precaution, I delay setting up my tent until dusk. I cook dinner with the burial sites a hundred feet away. I think about the people who lived and died in this area. The stories they had to tell, the storms of life in sickness or day-to-day trials or the real storms of hurricanes that interrupted their lives. Maybe they endured what I have endured on the trail, like mosquitoes and bloody feet and carrying water for miles in the heat of the day.

When the sun drops and darkness begins to overshadow the land, I set up my tent. It's a quiet but cold night, and I sleep well. The following morning I post on Facebook about my first time camping in a cemetery with the words, "I rested in peace." This prompts other observations from fellow commenters such as:

No body stirring to disturb you.

In the dead of night?

Sounds like a grave decision on your part.

Usually you have to make reservations at cemeteries—people are just dying to get in.

I get a snicker out of these. Followers on social media are coming along with me on this journey. Social media has also helped plan out hikes, meet new people, and even receive help if I need it. On the Colorado Trail last fall, I hit a Facebook group devoted to the trail to inquire about a shuttle to a trailhead. Not half an hour later I got a ride without having to hitch. I'm also part of the Florida Trail group, on which we keep one another informed of trail goings-on and ways to help each other. It's how I connected with the trail angel, Randy, who came to my rescue during those cold nights at the beginning of the hike and led to a glorious stay in an apartment. I set up with another hiker I found online, Nancy, who is keeping one of my resupply boxes farther up the trail. Social media allows one to stay connected with people you might not otherwise meet in life and to those who open their doors and their hearts to help in times of need.

Today finds me navigating mostly quiet gravel roads. I also meet people and dogs along the way. One hound follows me for quite a while until I finally turn and order him home. He stops in his tracks, hangs his head, and whines. I could've had quite a pack of would-be trail dogs for this venture—from the notorious Baxter to Bruiser who followed me until I met the prison detail, to this pup who thinks it's his job to leave home and be my companion. Dogs dearly want human companionship and adventure unless they are wired to protect their owner's domain. Most of the loose dogs have a wandering spirit and want only to explore and follow a friend. I think of my pooches back home, keeping Papa Bliss entertained, and likewise these pups who have kept my mind busy and away from the tediousness of road walking.

Now a pickup truck pulls alongside me. The man and woman inside remind me of a scene from the movie *Planes, Trains and Automobiles*—when the couple stops to assist Steve Martin and John Candy. I'm half expecting the man to get out of the truck and order his wife to pick up my backpack and help me. Instead the man asks how in the world I can be doing this hiking thing by myself.

I'm not one to broadcast that I'm hiking alone, though it's quite obvious there's no one else around. To most this would seem a fearful prospect. There are dilapidated houses in areas, and strange folks and dogs roaming about, and here I am trudging along, a solo female hiker, carrying a backpack. Thankfully I've done quite a bit of roadwalking already, but still I need to remain on guard. I know too that even if it appears like I'm alone, I know I'm not. Already God has dispatched an angelic army numerous times on my behalf. They have done their duty in protecting me from the trials and tribulations inherent in trail life. So I inform the man I'm a praying person, and I don't believe I'm alone.

He shakes his head. "That's all well and good, but if you're in trouble, the Lord ain't about to drop a four by four from the sky to help you out."

I honestly don't remember how I responded to his statement. Of course, many things enter my mind now, like the mere fact that God could very well drop a four by four in my path if He wanted to. He's God, after all. The Creator of the Universe. He rose from the dead and walked through doors to greet His followers. He burned a bush without singeing it and closed the mouths of lions. Which is comforting to a hiker walking in pure wilderness among the animal kingdom. I'm fairly certain I give the guy the impression I'm unconcerned about solo hiking and happily walk on. I never considered needing a rescue trailside, even though I've come close. Like last year when I wondered if I'd need a forklift to dig me out of that black pit of sucking mud. I hope this encounter isn't some kind of premonition of things to come. Quite frankly, I don't need it or want it. I summon faith instead and try not to sweat the stuff where I have no control. I'll let God handle it. For now, I'll just keep walking.

A few miles later I'm greeted by yet another pickup truck. The driver is in his mid-twenties, clad in plaid like a lumberjack, with his faithful pooch occupying the passenger seat beside him. I've been hearing sounds of machinery ahead of me in the woods and figure that's where his job site is located. He's now staring at me and my backpack as if I'm an alien before solemnly declaring, "Woo wee. In all the years I've been working here, I ain't never seen no one walk this here trail."

I step back, slightly startled. I realize that folks hiking the Florida Trail are few and far between. What amazes me though is this guy actually knows the trail runs along this road! I hate to think how many folks have no earthly idea what the Florida Trail is, that it is a National Scenic Trail, or that it even winds past their homes, through a town, along highways, or skirting the edge of a forest. I don't recall now what I said to him either, but he drives on to his lumber job. I soon run into his truck parked at the job site and his pooch wandering around, waiting for him. The dog decides I'm far better company than the lumberjack and follows me a good distance along the road. After about a mile I finally instruct the pooch to go home. He looks at me rather sadly, for he's been enjoying the excursion, then offers a doggy shrug and heads back to where his owner is hard at work harvesting timber.

For my final night on the road, I locate an obscure patch of woods and set up my tent. I relish the complete solitude, with no homes or cars or cemeteries or dogs or guys zooming around in pickup trucks or anything else. No one knows I occupy these woods, save God alone. It's peaceful and quiet, much like the cemetery. No matter where I am, God is there, holding me in His hand. It gives me reassurance that no matter what happens, I will be okay, because I trust in His holy name. And that is a comforting thought as I drift off to sleep, praying against any anxiety for what tomorrow may bring.

And according to the forecast on my phone, things are not looking good weather-wise....

CHAPTER ELEVEN

BLESSED ARE THE FLEXIBLE

AUCILLA SINKS AND THE ST. MARKS NATIONAL WILDLIFE REFUGE

Weather is on the brain this morning as I arise to find overcast skies. Fortunately the main batch of rain isn't expected to arrive until later in the day, which gives me time to hike the next section of trail, the Aucilla Sinks.[17] When I first heard of sinks in Florida, it dredged up a sad memory of news a long time ago, of a sinkhole that occurred in the middle of the state, swallowing whole a man and his house. The state rests on a virtual plate of limestone or rock composed of calcium carbonate, produced from dead marine life and coral that has solidified through time. This type of rock is easily eaten away by water to form holes like the ones encountered in the Big Cypress Swamp, the formations flanking the Suwannee River, sinks, and caves.

Back home, Papa Bliss and I explored the rich limestone areas of western Virginia with its many caves. Because it is not at sea level like Florida, in West

---

[17] Rumor has it the Florida Trail may eventually be moved away from these interesting geological features and closer to the coast.

Virginia the streams and rivers running through the limestone create the deep caves for some fun exploration. I recall one such adventure as a newly engaged woman, enthralled by my fiancé, whom I duly wanted to impress with my adventuresome spirit. Outfitted in the dingiest clothes I could find, as caving is a muddy venture, with a hard hat and light, we ventured into Marshall's Cave. This is not like a commercial cave of paved walkways to view the stalagmites and stalactites and snowball rooms and majestic chambers like Luray Caverns in Virginia, Mammoth Cave of Kentucky, or Carlsbad Caverns of New Mexico, all of which I have visited. Marshall's Cave is a purely primitive experience. The only light you see is the one you're wearing, hence the reason you must carry two light sources should one fail, along with lots of extra batteries. We gingerly made our way through the dark interiors until we could go no farther, observing the holes and pits created by the streams. I came out muddy and alive and able to say, *Yes, I am an adventurer.*

Now on the Florida Trail, I'm looking forward to seeing these limestone sinks. Reading up on what lies ahead, the trail guide warns of holes and sinks that can easily trip you up or turn dangerous should you slip in wet conditions. I think about all that rain heading my way and decide to try and hike the entire section in one day. I had intended to camp in the Aucilla Sinks area, but I don't want to be in some dangerous situation with rain beating down and my foot slipping and falling into a sink. That is not the way I wish to be remembered.

I celebrate the end of the fifty-mile roadwalk, eager to reenter the woods and onward to the famous sinks. Except when I do enter the woods, the orange blazes suddenly disappear. Here I am, happy to not be inhaling exhaust or entertaining questions by passersby in trucks or the wagging tails of canine companions following me, and now there's no trail to follow. I never thought I would miss a roadwalk where the ease of the journey is in knowing the route.

Thankfully I've been through the lost trail syndrome, à la the Allegheny Trail of West Virginia back in Chapter Two. I know how to look for trail traces and obscure trail blazes.

As I work my way toward the Aucilla River, I end up in thick forests of palmettos and blowdowns of various sizes. It's some of the worst trail conditions I've come across on the trail. For several miles I bushwhack my way through the tangled web of palmetto fronds, almost expecting Tarzan to come bursting out or see monkeys swinging from the trees.

When I come to a cleared path and brightly painted blazes, it's easy to see where one maintainer's section begins and the other ends. But to whom am I to complain? The maintainers of the Florida Trail are volunteers who give their blood, sweat, and tears to come out on their own and care for the trail. They have to haul in long and short clippers, chain saws, and other tools to their sections of trail and clear the way for hikers. Having worked in the woods as a ridgerunner on the Appalachian Trail, assisting hikers and doing some light trail maintenance, I know a little about a maintainer's life. I have the utmost respect for them and encourage those who love hiking to head to the nearest trail organization and volunteer to pick up a clipper and join a trail maintaining party. You make new friends while caring for God's creation so others can enjoy it. And I know I've experienced the satisfaction of clearing a multi-limb blowdown and watching the trail materialize before my eyes. It's a great feeling.

The trail eventually opens up to views of the Aucilla River, and then suddenly the flowing water is swallowed up by the earth. This is the fascinating feature of the Aucilla Sinks, reminiscent of the Lost River—a well-known geological feature of my time spent in West Virginia where the river disappears underground. The trail guide describes this section of the trail as littered with many large and small limestone holes or sinks. They appear like rocky bowls where the river pops out of its cavernous route for a greeting before disappearing once more into the earth. Each sink has unique characteristics. Some appear like caves with an invitation to go spelunking. Some are sinks without water but instead, display small cypress knee groves reminiscent of a fantasy world for gnomes and elves. I have to keep reminding myself that yes, this is still the United States. Witnessing such geological wonders, it's plain to see why the Florida Trail has a National Scenic Trail designation. It is a world

A place for elves and gnomes it seems
in this cypress knee grove in the Aucilla Sinks

unlike any other and one a hiker must experience to truly appreciate.

Late that afternoon I exit the sinks and prepare for a rainy go of it that night. The weather radar is indicating a mixture of bright yellows and reds heading in my direction. So far the weather on my hike has been pretty good. I can hardly complain. But whenever I see things that look to bring discomfort, I admit I wonder what will happen and if I'm ready for it. And no one I know likes getting soaked on a hike.

Interestingly enough, I deal with a half hour of the wet stuff, just enough for a nicely damp tent but with time in the morning to pack everything up. After many trail miles under my belt, I can safely say I've done my share of setting up and taking down in downpours. It's not fun, but it happens. So when I can catch a break in those reds and yellows of a major storm, I'll take it with gladness. Still I make sure my gear is in good bags—I use cuben fiber stuff sacks and a large trash bag to store everything in—and keep the rain jacket handy.

Now it's a few miles of roadwalking to the doorstep of the St. Marks National Wildlife Refuge. Roads are used to link section to section for much of the Florida Trail, so I continue to walk them from time to time. Along the way the rain starts to pick up, and I don my jacket and a big rain hat to keep the raindrops off my glasses. I know there's the potential for heavier stuff later on and decide to adjust plans accordingly. I opt to stay at the first campsite in the wildlife refuge which also happens to correspond with the campsite I registered for many weeks ago. The St. Marks National Wildlife Refuge requires hikers to reserve campsites ahead of time. It can be a challenge trying to figure out where you will be on a given date. For this reservation, I called the refuge ahead of time to plan it out. The patient ranger tried to tell me my mileage was off for my reservations, but I thought, *Hey, I know what*

I'm doing; I can read a mileage chart in the trail guide.
But no, I hadn't read it right and inadvertently planned
a twenty-plus-mile day between campsites. Another call
to the office and another e-mail corrected the situation.
Now many weeks later, the dates and campsites listed on
my permit are falling into place with my location on the
trail, and that's pretty amazing.

Right now though my stomach is rumbling, and I'm
eager to stop at the grocery store coming up to purchase
some snacks, a cold lemonade, and much needed water
before I enter the wildlife refuge. When I arrive, to my
sadness, the place is closed on Sunday. Which is good
in a way—they respect the day most go to church—but
disappointing to a hungry hiker. I will need to conserve
my food until my next town stop in two days. At least
I do locate the outdoor sink to fill my water bottles...
unfortunately from the warm tap as there isn't a cold
water handle. But it's needed. I'm entering an area with
an unknown availability of useable water sources due to
salt water contamination. This could get interesting.

*   *   *   *   *

There's always a sense of accomplishment when
one enters the next segment of the hike. The St. Marks
National Wildlife Refuge is known for a variety of wildlife
including numerous alligators, birds, and mammals. It's
also close to the Gulf of Mexico, which adds another sense
of accomplishment, having hiked from the northernmost
reaches of the Panhandle to just a mile shy of the Gulf, and
all by foot power. I enter the refuge to greet four happy-
go-lucky guys heading out. They're on a section hike—
that is, hiking a portion of trail in a given time period.
I've seen little in the way of backpackers on the Florida
Trail. It's nice running into them and chatting about
their experiences. They also come bearing fair warning

that there is no drinkable water anywhere in the refuge. Everything is brackish, they say. That is, tainted with salt. I thank them for the information and hurriedly scan my trail guide for any useable sources. I know the water I got from the convenience store will not last through tomorrow. The trail guide had warned me about sources being invaded by saltwater, rendering them useless. I will need to test any water I find to see if it's salty or not. I sigh and hike on, hoping for the best, knowing I may need to bang a staff on the ground as Moses once did to get any liquid reward.

I soon come upon a boggy area and see water in the middle of it. Grabbing a cup, I gingerly walk out to do a taste test. To my relief it's not salty, albeit a dark tannic color and likely fresh water from a past rainfall. It's tedious effort to dip out several liters for my camping needs, and the yellow color is hardly appealing. But it's drinkable, and that's all I care about.

With the dark drape of clouds thickening in the skies, I hasten to the first campsite in the refuge, Pinook Campsite, nestled in a grove of lovely palms and palmettos and beside an inviting stream. Except the water is salty and completely undrinkable. Still it's a nice spot, complete with little benches. I set up my tent and check the weather to see a huge storm coming my way. Although it's only one o'clock, I'm glad I decided to stop for the day and end up battling several rounds of intense rainfall in my little tent. I catch a break at dinnertime to venture out and cook a meal by the little bench. Because of the rain and falling temperatures in the area, the normally mosquito-infested site remains bug free. I know also those lovely boggy areas dotting the trail will now have fresh water in them to replenish my water bags. So there are advantages to stormy weather. But I also enjoy the pretty palms in my campsite, a day in paradise even with the rain, and look forward to what tomorrow will bring.

The next morning the weather is perfect for a walk through a national wildlife refuge, except the wind is blowing and it's actually quite cold. That doesn't keep a neighboring bobcat from scooting across the trail to welcome me to the wilds of a refuge where birds, reptiles, and mammals live and roam freely. But now I'm concerned that what I'd like to see most, the alligators, may find it too chilly for sunbathing. I walk across an open levee built up to access this part of the refuge, overlooking a wide estuary where fresh water meets a saltwater environment. It gives the hiker a taste of a new and different world. I gaze upon endless sawgrass prairies leading to two palm trees in the

The estuary at St. Marks National Wildlife Refuge

distance that no doubt front the great Gulf of Mexico. It's exciting to see this picturesque sight, realizing how far I have walked to get here.

Hiking on the levee that is exposed to all the elements, I'm glad I decided yesterday to stop early at the little protected campsite in the grove of palm trees. The next camping area is perched on an adjoining levee overlooking the estuary, covered in sand, making it a wet and sticky place in the rain. The "blessed are the flexible" beatitude in stopping early had definitely worked out to this hiker's advantage.

On the next levee is supposedly Gator City, USA, where one can spot many of the reptiles. I glance about to see if any are braving the chill, but it's windy and cloudy and no one seems interested in coming out of the nice warm water to see me. I finally spot two gator friends side by side, deciding there's just enough sun peeking through the clouds to welcome me to the wildlife refuge. I take pictures and thank them for making a chilly appearance just for me. They are the only two alligators I see in the entire refuge.

Reaching a park road at the next trail junction, an SUV drives by then suddenly makes a U-turn in a parking area and returns to stop beside me. The couple, wearing bright smiles on their faces, greet me, and tell me how they have just came from Shell Island Fish Camp near the St. Marks village, the very place I planned to stay. The husband then relates his own Florida Trail experience from several years ago. They produce a juicy apple—which I accept with grateful thanks—and offer encouragement for my journey. Munching on the tart goodness of fresh fruit, I relish the trail magic—which are unexpected acts of benevolence bestowed on a hiker by trail angels. The encounter gives a new lift to my step, as I've grown weary from the lengthy miles and the rising humidity. Especially as I have a due date with a boat taxi to take me across the St. Marks River and my stay at the Shell Island Fish Camp.

Glancing at my watch, I try to decide what time I'll likely arrive for the boat shuttle. It's an important calculation to make, for when I arrive at the river's edge, there's no other way across. No bridge, no ferry, no ability to wade, nothing. One must rely on either flagging down a boat or calling the Shell Island Fish Camp for a shuttle. Since I made reservations to stay at the camp, they offer to take me across the river for free, provided I arrive no later than four P.M. From the looks of things, I'm guessing my shore time arrival at three P.M. and place the call to let them know.

But just in case I run into obstacles that slow me down, which happens more often than not out here, I hasten down the trail composed of wide, sandy roads, hoping to make some time. I pass forests that have suffered prescribed burning, with the telltale signs of charcoaled ground and blackened tree bark. The St. Marks National Wildlife Refuge performs many prescribed burns, which is another reason they want hikers to obtain permits— so they know where they are at any given time. The prescribed burns have not yet affected me except for camping by roasted vegetation, and I hope it isn't going to be an issue farther along the trail. The burns in Ocala National Forest with pines charred at their bases and palmettos burnt to a crisp did not lend itself to a scenic jaunt. But I realize they're done to manage undergrowth that can root out certain tree specimens and as a way to curb wildfires.

I continue in haste to the St. Marks River, and in a short time I see a large sign and a ten-foot drop right into the river. Here the trail abruptly ends opposite the village of St. Marks. A few boats parade on by, hardly enough for a hiker to try and flag one down as an alternative to securing a shuttle. Secretly I'm glad I arranged for a ride. It makes life much easier. The only detail I wonder about is how I will actually get into the boat. There's no dock here, and it's a steep drop-off to the river. In preparation for it, I take off my shoes, tie them to my pack, and don my water shoes. I consider what else might get wet and try to ready myself for possibly submerging into the water when the boat arrives. The mere thought makes me pace and rub sweaty hands on my shorts. I do hope when Blissful the Hiker enters the boat, it will not go down as another twisted foible of the hike.

My water taxi arrives, and the boat captain expertly maneuvers the bow of his vessel right up to ground level so I can easily step into the boat. No fuss, no muss, no getting wet. I couldn't have asked for a better situation. After he takes my picture, I settle in for my one and only boat ride on the Florida Trail. The captain shares tales of life in St. Marks—from the hurricanes[18] that have blown through, to the tourist season and the town's history. I enjoy the journey while watching us motor along the shore, seeing a part of Florida from a different perspective.

Arriving at our destination a half hour later, I plan on spending two days at the Shell Island Fish Camp. St. Marks is my first major town stop on this leg of the Florida Trail, and all the chores of a typical zero, no hiking day are in order. I find out where the laundromat is, load up my backpack, and head out to walk the mile roadwalk to it. Along the way the friendly proprietor of the fish camp stops and gives me a ride to the facility. I love these little acts of kindness. With the task done in rapid fashion, I head to town for a bite to eat and to purchase a few groceries. With the weather cold and it being mid-week, the place is a proverbial ghost town. I get my choice of tables in the restaurant to enjoy a grouper sandwich and sweet potato fries with a view of the river and across the way, the prominent Florida Trail sign where I picked up the boat taxi the day before. No boats are on the river, making me glad I didn't try to flag down a boat ride today. It definitely pays to plan, at least where calling for a boat taxi is concerned.

I end the afternoon with a stop at a quaint grocery

---

[18] St. Marks and many areas of the Panhandle suffered major damage from Hurricane Michael in 2018.

store that reminds me of a bygone era with an elderly lady manning the antique cash register who invites me to sign the grocery store register. Then it's a peaceful walk along a bike path which is also the Florida Trail to intersect the road heading back to the fish camp.

The rest of the day I lounge around, repack my food, and ready myself for the last section of the wildlife refuge and on into Apalachicola National Forest. While I do enjoy the niceties of town, eventually it turns boring, with nothing to see and do except eat and sleep. Maybe this is why I never could be termed a homebound person but rather enjoy taking trips and seeing things. And it's time for more trail sightseeing into places unknown.

* . * . *

Returning to the trail, in a few miles I veer off the bike path and through a wild construction zone that herds me into an overgrown field of brambles, briers, pointy sandspurs, and yes, wet feet. Memories of pleasant days are short-lived as I attempt to muddle through this hurtful snag of brush tearing at tender skin. The trail eventually dumps into tamer ground, and suddenly with a click of my hiking poles and my nicely callused feet, I am transported into the most beautiful grove of towering palm trees I've seen on the trail. It's called the cathedral palms, and I can see why—the palms rise like mighty spires to embrace the sun. The grove of thick, plush, pristine trees are a vivid reminder of the great beauty and uniqueness that puts the Florida Trail in a class by itself. Along with thinking you've taken a side trip to some island in the Pacific, which is a nice thought.

A brief check shows my water is running low, so I head down a side trail to Shepherd's Spring, a pretty area rumored to be inhabited by a large alligator. I arrive to see a teal-tone body of water, warm to the touch, like a thermal spring. There is no sign of the gator, though I carefully scan the area for any eyes observing me. I take out my cup to check the water and to my dismay find it brackish and undrinkable. How sad. The Gulf waters have penetrated this far inland to infiltrate the spring. Now I must find another boggy place of fresh water, full of things growing in it, but such is life.

I spend the last night in the wildlife refuge at Wakulla Field Campsite on ground laced with pointy prongs of vegetation from recent bush hogging that could easily puncture both tent floor and sleeping pad. Not a comforting way to spend the night. The final day of walking in the wildlife refuge is actually spent on roads. The boardwalks constructed in a swamp-filled section of trail have floated away under the power of past tropical systems, and with dire warnings of sucking mud if you decide to venture through, I hit the detour. At least this route brings me to a convenience store where the cheerful clerk, with many a good story to tell, agrees to watch over my pack while I buy some food. If a roadwork can bring you to food and drink and some interesting conversation, it's not too bad of a detour. I'm glad also that, when I head back up the road to where the trail intersects, it will signal the end of another section and the beginning of the next.

Except I'm entering an area I've been dreading since this part of the trip began. And the anxiety returns anew....

CHAPTER TWELVE

THE SWAMP THING, THE SEQUEL

APALACHICOLA NATIONAL FOREST

An avid moviegoer who finds a particular film captivating will wait impatiently for the coming sequel to discover what happens. You've seen the main event, know the characters and their circumstances, and now you want the big finale. The Florida Trail has its own idea of the main trail movie event, *The Swamp Thing* in the Big Cypress National Preserve with several days of wading in murky water and finding one's way around limestone holes and cypress knees. The Panhandle offers hikers Bradwell Bay, or *The Return of the Swamp Thing*. Except this is one movie where I don't care to experience a sequel, thanks.

When I first began reading up on the second half of the trail, I spent the most time agonizing over Bradwell Bay in the Apalachicola National Forest. First, it's a mini Big Cypress with a trek through swamp water in a wilderness that's home to giant cypress trees. Second, I would have to do this part alone. Third, I wondered how deep it was and how wet I'd get. Fourth...would I survive? Fifth, should I take the bypass and save the anguish? Sixth, if I take the bypass and skipped it, I would probably regret it. Seventh, how can I call myself a hiker of the Florida Trail if I allowed this part to get to me? Lastly, stop with the questions and doubts and take whatever comes.

So what spurred this doom and gloom? I read some pretty intense descriptions in the trail guide ahead of time that infiltrated my brain and stirred up emotional responses. Like:

> *The Bradwell Bay Wilderness is the most challenging hike you'll encounter outside of Big Cypress, a wade through tannic waters into an ancient swamp forest that will take all day to traverse.*[19]

> *Except on rare occasions when the swamp dries out, you will get wet crossing this section. Water depths of waist high are normal. Allow plenty of daylight for your hike, as it involves a lot of scrambling over submerged logs and pulling your feet out of mud holes. The deep water section is 3.9 miles long and will take, at best speed, a mile an hour to cross. Hike with a companion if at all possible. Use a wooden stick for balance as the footing is unstable and each step ahead of you must be probed so you don't fall into a deep hole.*[20]

I had visons galore of stumbling into those deep dark holes or falling over a log with no one there to pick me up. I saw myself dragging my backpack out of hip deep water, with everything soaked and possibly ruined. All

---

[19] Sandra Friend and John Keatley, *The Florida Trail Guide* (Cocoa: Watula Press, 2017), 239.

[20] Friend and Keatley, 248.

this added up to a nightmare that I didn't think I could mentally handle. Which goes to the crux of all hikes—the mental game. I've spoken of the mental aspects of a hike many times as I write, speak, and share on online forums, the idea that any hike, no matter how long or short, is a mental game one must play to win. Most hikers like to concentrate on the physical aspects of a journey. Am I strong enough to hike the miles carrying a backpack? Sure, there are the physical aspects, but the emotional aspects of feeling cold, wet, vulnerable, hot, fearful, confused, frustrated, bored, homesick, all play into the mental game and whether the hike will succeed or not. Do you possess the mental fortitude to carry on, despite the emotional and even spiritual baggage that can weigh you down more than a loaded backpack itself? Can you keep going even when the going gets tough?

There I was, facing vivid descriptions of holes and water and mud and logs and getting lost and all those mental images that can elevate the anxiety level and curtail one's goal. Social media documents hikers refusing to even try the Florida Trail because of the walk in water. But God has a vested interested in water walking. The whole concept of walking on water is a foundation of faith. Peter nearly had a major crisis when Jesus commanded that he come join Him on the water. Can you imagine the actual sight of a man walking on top of the water? I would think I'd seen a ghost. An alien being. One of the Avengers. But when Peter calls out to Jesus, He says that Peter can likewise walk on water. So what did Peter need to accomplish this? Faith. He had to gingerly put his sandal (or probably a bare foot) on the greenish blue water. And then the most difficult part—standing and putting out the other foot. Wow. Talk about a leap of faith, from boat to water, and if anything goes wrong, you'll probably drown.

So despite all the visions I am faced with in Bradwell Bay, I'm fairly certain God doesn't want me to take a shortcut and skip it. What kind of a faith walk is that, especially after all I've been through? Even with the anxiety, I made plans for swamp trip number two and hoped I could walk on top of water and mud without tripping over logs or falling into holes.

Then I read some good news even before I left to hike the panhandle—a firsthand account on a trail forum of a hiker who has passed through Bradwell Bay unscathed. The hiker articulated that the swamp was virtually dry except for some muddy parts. There are apparently no issues at all. Hurray! Here I'd made the decision to go for it, and God met me by drying the place out. Praise be.

* . * . *

I begin my foray into Apalachicola National Forest teeming with confidence after the information shared about a dried-out swamp, even if the news is weeks old. I figure there's been no appreciable precipitation since the online report that could change the status of Bradwell Bay. There have been a few rainy days but not too bad, except for that one afternoon I spent in my tent in the St. Marks National Wildlife Refuge. But one day of moderate rain could not have changed things that drastically. I'll also be hitting the area at a good time, before the next major rainstorm is set to arrive.

Just in case, though, there's one final indictor of water depth within Bradwell Bay at a place called Monkey River. I wonder how people choose the names for these places. Maybe somewhere around here monkeys have been spotted. Who knows? Anyway, the water for Monkey River flows out of Bradwell Bay, so if the river is high, the bay is flooded and too dangerous to safely navigate. I check it out, and the river is only ankle deep. Though the crossing here is tricky, and I end up with wet feet for my trouble, it looks good for proceeding into Bradwell Bay.

A short distance away I set up camp in a flat space amid the brambles and thick vegetation. I try to relax and think on good things before the swamp sequel greets me the following day.

* . * . *

In the morning there's a thick layer of frost on my tent and clouds of smoke from my breath. It's downright cold out, and today of all days I plan on walking in a swamp. Not a pleasant prospect. At least in the Big Cypress National Preserve I had hot weather in which to traverse the watery trail. But there is danger of hypothermia if one gets too wet and chilled on a day like today. I prepare for it as best I can. My main focus is getting through it and praying the swamp is still semi-dry as first reported many weeks ago.

The first half of Bradwell Bay is a jumble of downed trees to climb over. At least it's dry here, except for a few muddy areas. I try to imagine having to negotiate these blowdowns in knee-deep water. It would have been impossible. So far things are going well, and I've decided the information received about the dry conditions is still accurate. Perhaps all the sweating and lamenting and downright anxiety had been for naught.

I pass the Bradwell Bay campsite, happy I did not make that my destination the night before. The area is completely overgrown with nowhere to rest one's head, let alone pitch a tent. Planning by way of intuition pays off, along with listening to that still small Voice telling you where to go, so long as anxious thoughts don't crowd it out. I'm feeling better about it all and turn my attention to the gigantic cypress trees looming above me. Their grandeur amazes me. It's easy to see why the forest received a wilderness designation, putting it off limits to loggers and protecting these huge specimens. Swamps do have their good points when they offer a safe haven for such a beautiful grove of trees.

Suddenly I see the trail shimmering before me, reflecting the clear sky. Swamp water, dead ahead. I look for places to skirt around the standing water using high ground, but no such luck. It appears that dry ground has finally run out. I succumb to the swamp sequel and enter the water, probing its depths with my hiking pole that nearly gets sucked out of my hand. I see also that in the middle of the supposed "trail" the water is nearly waist high, as the trail guide predicted. I stay to the edge as best I can to avoid the deepest parts, snaking my way through bit by bit, seeing how this could be a long and arduous process if the rest of the trail had been underwater. There's no clear water to see through either, like in Big Cypress. It's all muck and mire but thankfully only four-tenths of a mile long instead of over three miles.

Once I'm clear of the water zone, I breathe a sigh of relief, only to promptly lose my way when the trail takes some twists and turns. Searching out the map on my phone, I try to follow the arrow on the map app and navigate my way back through more blowdowns and brambles to the orange blazes. My anxiety level, once about a three in the water, is a raving eight in this jungle of hardwoods and cypress trees. When I finally stumble out of Bradwell Bay and onto an old forest road, I promptly sit down, peel off muddy socks to dry my feet, and proclaim victory over this part of *The Swamp Thing, the Sequel.* I'm none the worse for the trip, save a toenail that now falls off in protest. I'm happy it's over.

The next plan is lunch and a needed water stop at an old homestead called Langston Farm. There are limited historical experiences here on the trail, so investigating an old farm that illustrates the lives of those who eked out a living among the palms and swamps of Florida provides an interesting perspective on days gone by. Finding the farm's spring for a water fill-up proves a bit of a challenge, but I locate it behind a patch of bamboo and eat my lunch under the arms of a huge oak tree that stands guard beside the old homesite. I think about the family that once lived here and all they must have endured—the hardships, the joys, the heat and bugs, sickness, and tropical storms. Life and death came and went here, and now it's but a memory with just the shell of a home left standing as a silent reminder.

Returning to the trail, I enter the Ochlockonee River basin and another area subject to flooding as the trail comes close to this interesting river feature. But with the low water levels right now, there's no issue of that. Instead I continue to have major issues with losing my way in a tangled web of twisted trees and blowdowns. What the swamps do not do my mental state, losing the trail does. I should be long over the panic of it after enduring the Allegheny Trail in West Virginia and a few places here in Florida, but I'm not. At least this time I have a map on my phone with a trusty arrow to guide me. But it's a constant fight to keep my peace when anxiety and frustration, coupled with brief spurts of anger, seek to make me miserable. Then comes the onslaught of doubts. Why on earth am I subjecting myself to these conditions? Why am I even doing this? Who cares anyway?

When I emerge from the river basin, rattled at this testing in unknown places, at least I can confirm I'm still moving along the Florida Trail. But at the Porter Campground, a small area where car campers hang out to fish in the river, the trail once more eludes me. The campers here stare at this stranger arriving at their campground—the swamp monster from the great deep, legs and feet smeared with mud, hair standing in every direction, bearing the aroma of eau de hiker funk, and wearing a look of *I'm tired of getting lost.*

"You looking for the trail?" an older gentleman finally asks.

"Uh, yeah. It must be around here somewhere."

He points to some obscure path beside his camper, and I heave a sigh. I never would have found it without his help. They ask if I need water, bless them, but I tell them I'm good to go and thank them. Despite the outward appearances, people still look out for each other, even those carrying huge backpacks, trying to get from A to B to C. I feel better about everything as I press on.

Before me lies a dark, foreboding area, with the potent smell of burnt timber lingering in the air. It's a huge, newly-prescribed burn area, the ground pitch black and possibly still warm from the fires for all I know. I reach a bridge that spans a modest creek and head across it, only to find the fire has burned away the last section of the bridge, including the stairs. I look down at the fifteen-foot drop and think, *Okay, how do I get down from this thing?* I take off my pack and drop it to the ground then gingerly use the metal beams that survived the fiery ordeal to lower myself down. With charcoal-stained hands to match the woods, I venture on, but with the lateness of the hour, I realize I'll be camping in this blackened forest.

I set up my tent among broiled palmettos and the tainted bark of huge pine trees. I also prepare for rain, as it's supposed to hit any time now. So much for another adventurous day. I still have more to go in the national forest, complete with discovering the native bushes called titi, rounds of sucking mud, bogs and bog bridges of different types, and all those glorious things that make Apalachicola National Forest a one in a million place. But that is all for the future. Tonight I snuggle in my bag, having survived Bradwell Bay and the lost hiker syndrome of *Peter Pan's* lost flock, caught in some tropical paradise of tangled blowdowns and swamps. It's time to hunker down in the charcoal forest and await a new tomorrow.

* . * . *

The day is overcast with some rain during the night but no rain falling when I tear down the campsite. Packing up in pouring-down rain is like an acrobatic feat in double time to spare one's gear from total saturation. I pack up quickly anyway, as I have no idea when the skies might open up, and then start walking. Suddenly I'm overtaken by another hiker, one of the few I've seen since the trail's beginning. She's a young gal who started way back at Key West on New Year's Day. I note the date of February 4th and wonder how in the world she can be here already from Key West! Some of these young folks put on miles like race car drivers of the feet and legs, with thirty-mile days her typical length. We chat for a few minutes. I note the tiny backpack she's carrying, more like a daypack really, and that she's wearing Chaco sandals. And just as quickly as she came, she disappears into the palmettos. I wonder if I might see her again, but at least now there's footprints to follow through the rest of this national forest, and at times they will help guide me when the trail takes abrupt turns.

The trail guide tells me I will be heading into areas occupied by titi or bushes with small teardrop-shaped leaves. To me the name conjures images of a Tahitian paradise with a scent of tropical fruit in the air. Instead I learn that when you see bushes of titi on the trail, it signals swamp, dead ahead. Titi thrive in wet conditions, so I brace myself whenever I encounter them, knowing it's going to be wet. Sometimes there are nice boardwalks to carry you over the wet places. Sometimes your feet must carry you directly into muddy areas, which the trail guide refers to as a gum swamp. I had my encounter with sucking mud in Ocala National Forest, so the phenomenon is not new to me. I try to minimize the impact by stepping on fallen trees or rocks to navigate around it. It helps also to see the footprints of the young hiker from Key West and where she goes to avoid the mud-filled areas. Though I can't imagine the feel of mud oozing between her toes, wearing those sandals.

Just as I'm making my way through the next swamp, the skies open up. Now I really feel like I'm in the Amazon jungle, pushing through walls of titi, slogging through sucking mud in a gum swamp, all in a heavy, tropical downpour. How's that for a picture that refuses to let you go? When I emerge onto some forest roads, muddy and soaked to the skin, the roads also exhibit the wrath of rain with gigantic puddles I need to circumvent. It appears any drought in the area is finally over. In Sapling Head Swamp I find yet another place drowning in water, but at least with a few logs to help me navigate. Until I attempt to cross a wet log and nearly fall off into the murky water below. I end up with nasty cuts on my legs from side branches. It jars my nerves enough that along with the ensuing battle of the swamp, I decide to call it quits for the day and find a nice dry campsite in some welcoming pine woods. It's been a tough go of it mentally, with yesterday's trek through Bradwell Bay and getting lost, and now slogging through titi swamps. But the sun is shining and there's a warm wind, perfect for drying out gear. With two pairs of socks now mud-soaked, and me included, I decide to make tomorrow's stop a paid campground so I can wash off both the socks and me. I string up a makeshift clothesline and dry most everything before the clouds roll in. It's a peaceful place to spend an enjoyable evening on the Florida Trail.

Struggling into still wet shoes and muddy socks the next day is not one of the fun parts of trail life. But at least my feet have toughened up enough to take the continued dampness for several days. By using trail runners, which are athletic shoes rather than full size hiking boots, the drying process begins when the sun comes out. My goal is the Camel Lake Campground, where I can relish potable water coming out of a faucet instead of drawing tannic water from a swamp, real restrooms, even a picnic table to cook on—all luxury items in a backpacker's world. The walking is made easier on boardwalks rising out of the mud and standing water, some a quarter mile in length, going under and over trees, and I can't help but applaud the trail maintainers who managed to build them.

Low bridge! Tree on the boardwalk through a gum swamp in Apalachicola National Forest

Today I encounter another couple out backpacking the Florida Trail, heading south—or rather, east across the Panhandle. The woman is wearing an interesting contraption, a backpack on wheels from a belt fastened around her waist that she drags behind her. She says she's had some difficult injuries in the past and this backpack-mobile affords her the ability to hike. I look at this half-cart, half-backpack in interest but wonder of its practicality. Especially in the latter part of the Apalachicola National Forest, going under trees on the boardwalk, slogging through gum swamps, and heading into Bradwell Bay and its game of pick-up sticks with the many blowdowns. But they are a fascinating couple to talk to, and I wish them the best on their venture.

Today is a short day of thirteen miles to the campground, arriving in midafternoon to find a blackened site from a fresh prescribed burn. Yes, the national forest personnel have burned out the campground, but it's open to the public. Campers are in residence, and the host bustles up to greet me and show me a site for the night. The air is pungent with the smell of smoke, and no semblance of living matter exists anywhere but for the people who come by to say hello. One woman in the site opposite mine stares at me with great sympathy. And suddenly she says, "Forgive me," and touches the cuts and contusions on my leg that I suffered in the Sapling Head Swamp. "Look at that! You need to take care of yourself and your feet there!"

I can't argue with her assessment, from the bleeding blisters to nails falling off, to fighting the battle of the trail in swamps and titi that test the will and batter the flesh. I spend the rest of the afternoon in the restroom, trying to rid myself and my socks of mud. I fear the entire sucking swamp may be forever embedded in the sock fibers, and they will never be the same. I use the hand blower to try and dry them some and return to my campsite. I'm getting hungry, and I have little food left after having hiking for several days. I kind of hope beyond hope that I might get some food, maybe from a sympathetic camper. But everyone stays hidden in their campers to cook and eat. I resort to a bowl of ramen noodles for dinner while envisioning the food I plan to buy at the next town. I thought my condition might drum up sympathy by way of a meal, or maybe a bag of chips, which I have a real hankering for. But I also appear to have my act together in the campsite with a clothesline strung, my tent set up, and me sitting at the picnic table, absorbed in a trail guide. I'm not exhibiting the art of yogiing very well, though the people across the way did offer me some coffee.

Next morning I head out before anyone in the campground stirs. These early morning hikes are the best with the subtle quietness of pine forests—even if they be blackened forests—and the sky turning from red to orange to aqua blue with the rising sun. I'm also giddy as this is my final day in a place that has been one of the more challenging sections of the Florida Trail. I'm glad the trail guide doesn't tell me what's ahead though, as this national forest will still pack a sound punch before I finally bid it farewell....

Such as crossing Sand Creek. With all the rain a few days ago, the creek has swollen considerably. From the bank I see something strange lurking underwater—a huge two-foot wide drainage pipe blocking the trail. I look for a way around it, but the water is at least waist deep if not deeper on either side of the pipe. I have no choice but to enter the river, climb on top of the massive pipe, and use it like an underwater bridge to cross over to dry ground. If it's at all slippery, my feet will fall right out from under me, I'll head underwater, backpack and all, and my final day in the Apalachicola National Forest will be a disaster.

My anxiety over the situation rises to a fevered pitch. *What am I going to do? What if that thing is slippery? I'm stuck! That's it. I can't do it.*

I put up one foot to test it. I lose my nerve and hastily withdraw. *This is impossible. Aren't things tough enough out here?* I guess I won't go through it all until I come to that wonderful sign at the northern terminus of the Florida Trail at Fort Pickens. Which right now might as well be in a galaxy far, far away.

Lauralee, just do it, I tell myself. And then I plead,

Please, please God, don't let me fall off this underwater thing!

I grunt and climb on top of the huge pipe. Praise be, it's not slippery at all, and I make my way across to reach some gnarly tree roots and solid ground once more. I look back at the underwater trap, unable to believe I actually climbed on top of some huge pipe wearing a backpack and walked across like a gymnast on a balance beam. I shake my head, thinking about it while passing through more watery places and holes hidden under the vegetation that could easily break an ankle. There are so many strange obstacles to overcome out here, I have come to believe the trail is a mental and emotional undertaking rather than anything physical. I agree with this assessment even more as I slosh through my umpteenth swamp-filled forest, reminiscent of a mini Bradwell Bay, in ankle deep water. It's now so familiar, I treat it as par for the course.

Finally I see the kiosk ahead of me, marking the end of the Apalachicola National Forest. Hoo-yah! And no, I'm not the least bit sad to leave. There's usually something good to recall on each section of trail, and maybe if I hadn't experienced a near meltdown at the gigantic underwater drainage pipe in Sand Creek, the hike here might have finished on a higher note. But right now, I can think of nothing good except to say—I did it, despite the swamp and titi and gum and sucking mud galore.

CHAPTER THIRTEEN

ANGELS ON THE HIGHWAY

THE CENTRAL PANHANDLE—PART ONE

The sight of a large Apalachicola National Forest sign on the road brings unparalleled joy to my heart. I bid the place a loud farewell with my feet soaking wet from the morning's encounters and move to the road that will lead me to the town of Bristol. Unfortunately wet feet, combined with warm roadwalking, makes the blisters return in force. My feet have endured so much on this hike, I'm actually amazed they're holding up as well as they are. I can't wait to take off my shoes to air out the wet toes and peeling soles of my feet, as soon as I reach the lovely convenience store described in my guidebook. I think about what food I want to buy there—maybe a hot dog, a cold soda, a bag of chips.

Arriving at the store, I venture in to find sodas scattered all over the floor, a two-year-old perched on a seat at the counter watching a cartoon, and the owner shouting every word of obscenity into his cell phone in front of the two-year-old. Meekly I grab for a bag of chips and soda, which he rings up without pausing in his raucous conversation. I leave the place shaking my head, sad for the little child exposed to such things, and with my eyes opened to a hard life for some folks. There is tough living in this world, with poverty in rundown shacks and little kids barefoot and dirty. It's a wake-up call for a hiker engaged in her own little hiking world where I've been living these many weeks to realize there's the reality of life beyond the trail.

But now a new issue crops up when I receive a text message from Papa Bliss. My upcoming mail drop may be lacking the medicine I need; and it's the one currently waiting for me in Bristol. It's a major resupply too, not just for medication but for picking up the new shoes that I desperately need. No medicine means I could be in a big hoodoo of trouble. I need to get to the post office posthaste. If I can verify there is no medicine, Papa Bliss will still have time to overnight me some. Besides, I could use those new shoes with feet blistering anew from wet, worn-out, funky footwear on hot sand and pavement. The sun is blazing, I'm tired, and I still have five miles to walk to town. I'm not happy about my situation, but there's nothing I can do.

Suddenly out of nowhere a car stops beside me. A woman smiles and holds out a cold bottle of water. I take it with thanks, think for a moment, then inquire if she's heading to town. I explain my predicament with the medicine and how I could sure use a lift to the post office to check on it. The woman, Randy, agrees to take me to town and then bring me back to complete my walk. Thanking God for this wonderful roadside angel, I enter the car, realizing I probably smell pretty bad from my multi day excursion in the national forest. But from her conversation, she is a kind and understanding soul who works with kids in the woods. In no time she gets me to the post office and waits patiently while I grab my mail drop. I discover the medicine *is* in the box as well as my new shoes, praise be, and return to the car with all the goodies for the next section of trail. She returns me to the pick-up point, for which I thank her profusely. Along the shoulder of the highway I repack my backpack with the food from the maildrop, now six pounds heavier, then heft it up to walk the remaining miles to town. When I notify Papa Bliss that I have the pills, courtesy of a trail angel who took me to the post office, he asks why I didn't just stay in town. Well...I've come too far through swamps and mud and storms and roads and titi and climbing on top of underwater drainage pipes and what-have-you to take shortcuts. He calls me crazy. I call myself determined to hike this entire thing, come what may.

On the way to town, I stop at another convenience store where they are just closing up the restaurant, but I manage to snag chicken strips and a big plate of fries. The meal plus some pink lemonade gives me the extra energy to huff the final miles to Bristol. On the outskirts of town, I pass by a school that has let out for the day, and students are making their way home. They look me over as some unique oddity out here with a pack on my back before two inquisitive kids finally ask what I'm doing. I tell them I'm hiking the Florida Trail. They have no idea what it is or that the trail even runs along the sidewalk in front of their school. I tell them they need to look it up on the Internet; that it starts near the Everglades and winds its way through the middle of the state and across the Panhandle to Pensacola, all 1,100 miles of it. They look rather puzzled before shrugging and pedaling away on their bikes toward home.

At last I trudge into Bristol, glad for the new shoes on my feet, and check into the friendly motel owned by a family from India. There's no laundry facility in town, and having stinky, muddy clothing from a week in the national forest, I *must* do wash. I strike up a conversation with the woman at the desk, mention my quandary about laundry, and tell her I will gladly pay. She looks at me, says they do have a washer, and I can give a donation for it. Great news! Later when my laundry is scheduled to be finished, I mosey on over to the laundry area to find a young man folding my freshly laundered clothes. He's of college age and talks about the motel business that has been in his family for many years. It's an interesting conversation about a family-run operation and the many hands that make it work.

I relax in town on a zero day of no hiking, except to run a few errands like mailing back my cold weather clothing and checking out the all-you-can-eat lunch spot in town. This place, with a buffet of fried chicken and all the fixings, plus bottomless glasses of iced tea, becomes my home for several hours. Everyone from town gathers here for lunch, and I out-sit three rounds of customers as I eat plate after plate of chicken, turnip greens, bowls of salad, and five pieces of cake with chocolate frosting. It's fair to say that hiker hunger has kicked in strong, besides the fact the food is great too. I waddle back to the motel just before it pours and, from the comfort of my room, watch the rivulets of water running down the windowpanes, thankful not to be out in it. I can just imagine trying to get through those special areas of Apalachicola National Forest in all this rain, like Bradwell Bay or Sapling Head Swamp or Sand Creek, and it's not a pretty picture. In fact, it could have been downright dangerous.

The phone and social media outlet continues to be the place for me to share my current adventures. I post pictures of the underwater pipe nightmare and the town stay with my plate of unending food. A fellow hiker, Robert, then offers to pick up the tab for my lunch that day. He got his money's worth for sure the way I gorged for two hours. I thank him for the kindness while quietly thinking how I've done nothing to earn the gesture. I'm just a hiker out doing a trail. Maybe the unexpected kindness is to show me that despite the bad that seems to get all the attention these days, it's much better to focus on the good and good-hearted people. Time to accentuate the positive rather than the negative. We don't have to do a laundry list of things either to receive favor. We get blessed even when we don't deserve it. It's called grace.

Now for the grace of the weather, which is looking a bit dubious for the upcoming week with rain forecasted the next few days. I'm insanely diligent to keep stuff dry and triple bag camp clothes, my sleeping bag, and other important items. I've been in all-day rain where everything gets soaked, even with a pack liner and a pack cover, and it's not pleasant. I do whatever is necessary to stay safe. Active thoughts about the upcoming hike keep me awake during the night. My next resupply is being held by a friend I met on an online trail forum, and with the date set for the rendezvous, I know there are long miles ahead to make it on time. I tend to get nervous about every new section, wondering what's in store. That's why I must stay focused on grace and strength for each new day and not worry about tomorrow.

* . * . *

The trail out of Bristol follows the road for the first few miles, crossing a 1.6-mile long bridge that spans the Apalachicola River and its surrounding swamps. It also marks the first time I will hike from the Eastern Time Zone to Central Time. I know that doesn't sound like a big deal to most, but for me, having crossed many state lines by foot, I'm now crossing time zones! A time zone change also means other things about the hike must change. Like the length of daylight in which to hike. In the morning I need to be out earlier and stop early in the day so I'm not caught in darkness or bug heaven. Instead of getting up at 6:15, I must arise at 5:15. Instead of arriving at camp no later than five P.M., I need to roll in by four P.M. The time change requires a different mindset so I can hike the miles I need while playing it safe.

Today the slanted shoulder along the roadway leaves much to be desired. My body dislikes carrying a fully restocked backpack tilted to one side. Stress develops on already worn-out joints. I look for ways to level out the walk while making sure I am not leveled off by speeding vehicles. At a road intersection sits a convenience store frequented by interesting people in pickup trucks, but I can't pass it up. I look for a place to stash my pack near a dumpster and head in for Doritos and lemonade, which are fast becoming my food and drink of choice at the market. I've always been partial to the tangy taste of lemonade on hikes. It seems to satisfy my thirst and energy level more than any other liquid beverage. Alternating with Doritos to fulfill the salty craving with a good cheesy flavor, it's a winning combination to my taste buds.

I exit the road now into the Chipola Wildlife Management Area, one of many wildlife management areas allowing trail access but also with active hunting grounds. All seems quiet on the hunting frontier, but I put blaze orange on my pack just in case. I work my way along the interesting Chipola River to an overgrown campsite that appears not to have been used in years. It works for me, because an isolated spot beside the peaceful sound of a river provides for one of my better night's rest.

Unfortunately, the quick ramble along a river and through the woods is short-lived, and the trail again diverges to assorted roads for the remainder of the day. For many hikers, the thought of roadwalking is one big reason the Florida Trail turns them off. As I've already described, roads give one an appreciation not only for how great the woods are when you're in them, but allows you to taste real Americana that one rarely experiences by car. Roadwalks also continue to net weird sightings in the garbage arena. This time it's assorted animal and bird parts (blech), an Ecco cake tin that appears brand new, socks, and a cowboy boot.

The paved road then turns to dirt and becomes more isolated. I check the map app for a side trip to another store, this time to pick up some garbage bags for the several inches of rain expected soon, along with more food. It's going to be a wet one, and I want to be prepared. I detour off the main trail to hike in a square formation that will net me a store stop and then a return back to the trail. The Family Dollar store affords the hiker cheap food options for resupply and a small carton of garbage bags. I can't help but go crazy in there, especially as I'm in the throes of unrelenting hiker hunger. And one knows they should *never* visit a food store on a growling stomach like I'm doing right now. I buy a lot of snacks and end up eating a decent chunk of it, sitting outside the store on the concrete sidewalk, feeling somewhat like a drifter. And people are eying me like I'm one, too.

Heading back up the main highway, I intersect the dirt road of the trail to head for the Econfina Section. On the way, I pass a couple walking along the road. The young woman is dressed in skimpy clothing and high heel sandals, and she tells me how much they love walking every day and how they've gotten lost in the Econfina area. I smile, inwardly hoping this is not a warning about trail conditions while wondering how she can walk in those sandals.

The Econfina section is one of the more interesting areas of the trail and rather rugged by Florida standards. It's similar to the Suwannee River with steep ups and downs as the river undercuts the terrain and forms bluffs, but framed by sweeping magnolia trees. Several elaborate bridges have been built across the river tributaries, and there's nice camping. I find a sweet spot near the Penny Bridge to set up for the night. It's been a long day, twenty miles hiked with the detour to the store, and I'm bushed. Again I wonder what tomorrow will bring with the weather outlook and a planned detour around a wide logging area, putting me on a network of forest roads and then an overnight stay somewhere along highway SR 20. None of this is very heartening to me, but neither is it good to try and figure out everything ahead of time.

The following day I enjoy more of the scenic Econfina Area with pretty river views and fairly substantial camping areas for those with reservations, complete with picnic tables and fire grates. I end up visiting one of these camping areas near Rattlesnake Pond, where I filter water for the rest of the day. I still have no idea where I'll spend the night, but I figure God will guide me to the right campsite out on the highway as He has in the past.

The Florida Trail now exits onto forest service roads to bypass a swath of heavily timbered land. The area looks like a bomb went off, with the land transformed to a moonscape devoid of all vegetation. It's like something you might see in an end times movie. The road detour adds several miles to my hiking total for the day, and I'm feeling it. Phone coverage has been poor today, so I've only left one text message for my trail angel, Nancy, who's holding my next resupply box. I'm scheduled to meet her sometime tomorrow and text her with the grittier parts of the day:

> *Thanks so much for everything you're doing. It's been just tough out here. I'm having to do long miles. But will take it one day at a time and can't wait to see you. You are a godsend.*

I recheck messages when I have cell service, and in comes a text from Nancy:

> *You need anything right now? I can come to you. Are you in Econfina yet?*

I text back:

> *I just did the bypass, I'm at SR 20. Hoping to make it a few more miles and then going to stealth[21] somewhere off SR 20. I'm done with Econfina.*

Her reply:

> *I can come get you so you can stay dry tonight and slackpack you tomorrow and Monday if you would like. I know we have nasty weather coming in.*

I stare at the text message, stunned. Did she just say she will come get me? A sudden tear creeps into my eye. I decide to call her and tell her it's too far to get me. But she is most eager to pick me up anyway, despite the ninety-minute drive from her home to my location. I think to myself how this is so not worth it for her. I inform her I will be okay and not to bother. But she insists it's no bother, so I agree, inwardly excited to be out of the rain and not camping on the side of a major highway. Nancy's kind of determination, mixed with compassion, and driving some one hundred miles to bail out a lone hiker, epitomizes the idea of "Think more highly of others than yourself" (Philippians 2:3). I have seen the kindness of angels here in Florida without a thought for themselves, and it's convicting.

I walk down SR 20 for several miles to the predetermined meeting place where we will link up. When I arrive at the spot, I sit there thinking about my time on the trail and realize how mind and body and emotional and spiritual

---

[21] *Stealth* is a term used by hikers to mean camping in a place where technically you may not be allowed and doing it discreetly. Normally I abide by the rules as best I can, but on the Florida Trail, one sometimes needs to do what is safe and practical.

aspects have all come through many stages in many situations. It's been a crazy but interesting journey of growth, with much more to come.

Nancy now buzzes up in her car, just as it starts to rain. We greet each other, and I thank her for coming all this way to help me. Then she says, "I thought you might be hungry," and points to a shopping bag. I stare, unblinking, at chicken tenders and a fruit bowl and other goodies. I can't believe she bought me food, nor can I believe how famished I am when the food quickly disappears. The lovely mixed fruit of watermelon, cantaloupe, blueberries, strawberries, and grapes are the epitome of a hiker fantasy. I feel like I have taken a side trip to the Candyland of food that hikers only dream about.

The ninety-minute trip speeds by, and soon I'm stepping into a nice home to greet Nancy's husband before heading to the shower to wash away the grime. Afterward I take a mini tour of the homestead/farm and a detached building dubbed the man cave, where Nancy's grown sons hang out. The man cave is complete with a mini kitchen, full bath, recliners, a table and chairs, a huge television, all the comforts of home but away from the main house. I'm introduced to the sons reconstructing the front end of a truck in the garage. It's great to see young men working together on a project, determined to see it completed. Hard work and effort are always greatly rewarded, and I can tell just by what I'm experiencing already that this is going to be a time of learning and appreciation.

The next morning I check the weather radar to see that copious amounts of liquid stuff are projected to fall in rain and heavy thunderstorms. At least I'll be slackpacking without carrying all my backpacking gear, and that's a relief. I'm also relieved that most of the bad weather appears to be dodging the area I'll be hiking in. We are getting some light rain now but nothing too bad. It should be an uneventful hike and then a nice return to this home away from home.

Nancy drives me another hundred miles back to the trailhead where I left off yesterday. There I take up my daypack and hiking poles. She stares at me solemnly before remarking, "You know how to reach me if things go wrong. I can pick you up most anywhere."

I thank her but assure her nothing is going to go wrong. I'm confident I won't need a rescue. I'm in this thing for the long haul. Come what may, I'm hiking this trail.

CHAPTER FOURTEEN

FARM LIVING IS A GOOD LIFE

THE CENTRAL PANHANDLE—PART TWO

With confidence I begin a new day—I've been helped along by a wonderful trail angel, feasted on wonderful food, spent the night in a wonderful bed, and made new friends with a wonderful family. It all must translate to wonder out here on the trail. I'm hiking this twenty-mile section with just a daypack and nothing to hold me back from reaching my goal. I hurry along for the first part of a seven-mile roadwalk. As the fine falling mist turns to a steady rain, I think deep thoughts while sticking close to the sides of the embankment to avoid the road spray of trucks zooming on by. When the coast is clear of traffic, I head for the pavement to make some time until headlights appear in the fog, and I quickly veer to the wet grass. Unfortunately, there are no powerline easements for me to follow, which can make the walking safer. I wish I could recall what occupied my mind during those long morning hours in the rain. But when the skies darken and the rain turns to a raging thunderstorm, my mind right now is on safety. I stop every so often to empty my pack cover that rapidly fills with rainwater. Trying to find a place to rest is a feat as there is no shelter anywhere; nothing but woods lining the road. It's an invariable no man's land along this major highway. Finally I head into a patch of pine, sit in front of a large tree with the rain beating down, and rapidly eat a granola bar I had slipped into the side pocket of my pack.

A new thunderstorm now begins to roar away, complete with lightning bolts zipping near electrical lines running along the left side of the road. The sight sends a shiver racing through me. I stick to the right side of the highway to avoid the hazard and meet another hazard by walking with the flow of traffic. What a choice—risk being hit by a car or electrocuted by lightning. When walking in storms like this, I wonder why on earth I'm doing this. Papa Bliss had actually urged me to stay out of the weather today and take a zero, especially as some weather reports indicated the possibility of nine inches of rain. But I couldn't see myself staying home when there's hiking to be done. I have a due date with Eglin Air Force Base so I will arrive on Presidents' Day weekend, which is quickly approaching. The long holiday weekend provides a narrow window to hike when the base is open to recreational use, and my permit is approved for those specific dates. I have little choice but to stay within my goals, come rain or wind or lightning. I reassured Papa Bliss as I did Nancy, that I will be fine. Papa rarely goes against my stubborn, can-do attitude. Which at times really should be can't-do, especially when confronted with the reality of a given situation. I'm not one to shirk safety though, as I do want to come out of this in one piece. I rely on that still small Voice to be my guiding light when hiking in tough conditions. And right now I don't hear anything telling me to stop.

A cheery double orange blaze alerts me that the trail is finally exiting the road I've been following for an eternity and now heads for a powerline easement. From what I can gather on the map app, searched quickly on my cell phone as the rain beats down, the trail runs for several miles underneath the powerlines before entering Pine Log State Forest. After reading the trail guide ahead of time, I'm already pensive about the state forest. It mentions several water crossings that can easily flood. And right now flooding is active from the heavy rainfall.

Suddenly a bolt of lightning zips down and hits the powerline directly above me in a loud crack of red and orange sparks. I let out a scream and start running, realizing full well I shouldn't be walking under proverbial lightning rods in an active thunderstorm. But I have no choice. It's crazy, I know, and I'm crazy for hiking in this.

After about a half mile, I encounter a wide rushing stream cutting through the easement. I stop dead in my tracks. I doubt this stream is ever running except in heavy rain, when low-lying places can easily flood. Now it's been raining for hours, setting up a flash flooding scenario that comes with the warning: *turn around, don't drown.* I look at the water before me and wonder how deep it is. After my adventures in Apalachicola National Forest, I have no qualms about wading. To a point. Using my hiking pole to test the depth, the water runs clear up to the handle, meaning this insignificant stream is at least waist deep. I look around for an alternate place to cross, but there is none. I know if this stream is flooded, surely the places pointed out in Pine Log State Forest in my trail guide will be as well. Reality is staring me in the face. I can no longer hike the trail here.

As difficult as this is, I turn around and look for the best way to return to SR 20. In adverse weather, a detour to bypass a hazard becomes the real trail. I faced a similar scenario on the Long Trail in Vermont when trying to climb Camel's Hump. With torrential rain and winds that sounded more like a freight train traveling at full speed, I knew I had no hope of making it over the hump that lies above treeline and is exposed to the full brunt of the elements. I took out my map to study it and decided on another trail to bypass the adverse weather wreaking havoc on Camel's Hump. The route led me around the base of the summit and exited on the other side where the Long Trail comes in just below the Hump. Up the trail I could hear the roar of wind on the summit, and I knew I had made the right decision.

Now I look at my map app and see a faint road trace that will lead me back to SR 20, though it requires some bushwhacking. As I do, I stumble upon a deer stand and huddle under the platform lurking above me. I call Nancy to let her know about the change in plans. She agrees to pick me up in Ebro at the gas station there. I'm not happy to be detouring around Pine Log State Forest, but with the relentless storms, it's better to alter plans than be swept away in a flash flood or be fried by lightning.

I reach the town of Ebro and the combination gas station and Subway, where I order a meatball sub. I feel like a drowned rat when I take off my rain jacket. Water streams off, forming a large puddle on the floor. I'm amazed and somewhat embarrassed at how wet I am and give the gal who made my sandwich an extra tip for flooding her store.

Nancy arrives like the cavalry to take me back to her house, and thankfully she brought towels so I wouldn't saturate her car. A party is in full swing when I arrive at the house, with the family gathered around to watch their favorite sports on television amid a bounty of food. Nancy is a cook who goes way beyond the call of duty, preparing feasts for her family every night. She is content to do it whether they eat it or not. I, on the other hand, need no urging to eat, especially after what I've been through. I look at the sumptuous buffet of barbecue chicken and hotdogs and salad with little containers of nuts and fruits and cheese to add to the salad, plus a big bowl of fresh fruit and pies. I wonder if the powerlines did strike me dead and I'm now in food heaven. While everyone else is glued to the television, I eat and eat and want to shout from the housetops how blessed they are and how blessed I am after a day spent in pouring rain with life literally flashing before my eyes. There are angels in life and there are angels with advanced degrees like the archangel type, and Nancy is well on her way to earning that supreme status in my book.

The next morning she rises at the crack of dawn, ready to whisk me back to Ebro, over an hour away, so I can accomplish a twenty-one-mile day to make up for yesterday's shortened hike. I ask about donating gas money for all these long road trips. She flatly refuses, and I slink down in my seat with an inward sense of wonder over this giving heart. I wish I could repay the kindness in some way, but sometimes it's better to receive than to give and allow the act to humble one's soul.

Before leaving, I checked the river flood gauge online to see if the next portion of the trail through the Choctawhatchee River basin is passable after the deluge. Nancy described some nice boardwalks built in this relocated part, but the river has indeed reached flood stage from the charts, putting the boardwalks under water. That means another ten-mile road detour, which is getting to be more common than not these days. I'm not happy to be missing the pretty Florida wilderness by having to take all these detours. At least I know, after hearing about trail maintainers chased out of Pine Log State Forest due to flash flooding, that I'd made the right decision yesterday to abandon the real trail and detour on the road. High water can't be helped but safety can, and the detours then becomes the trail, even if this is getting to be a little monotonous.

To add insult to injury, I start off by walking another two hours in rain with road spray dousing me from passing vehicles. Thankfully when I arrive in the sleepy town of Bruce, the weather has let up and there's even some peaks of sunshine to brighten my day. Maybe I will finally bid adieu to the dew and embrace some good weather in the days ahead. I don't think the trail or I can take much more precipitation.

After ten miles on the road, I enter with enthusiasm the Florida wilderness dubbed the Nokuse Plantation. When one thinks of a plantation, images of an antebellum Southern structure with a long front portico and columns, surrounded by large fields, come to mind. Actually this plantation is an area of conservation where longleaf pines are being reintroduced. I was forewarned on a hiker forum not to take the main trail running along Lafayette Creek, as it's likely flooded. I use a blue-blazed bypass route on a forest road that has seen its share of washouts. When I reenter the woods, I find substantial stream crossings with vast amounts of mud and gravel from major flooding. But a wet environment also means beautiful mushrooms are popping up everywhere. The forest of the Nokuse materialize in acre upon acre of longleaf pine, planted in nice straight rows, with the undergrowth burned to aid in their maturing. In these burned forests I feel like I'm walking through a nether world amid black pools of water like a woods oil spill. Dodging these boggy areas, I envision the thought of walking on water rather than sinking in them. Many tributaries and streams are still fairly swollen with evidence of even greater flooding during yesterday's deluge. In certain places the footbridges themselves are swamped or curiously floating atop the creek, positioned over the deepest parts. To see a person standing on a footbridge surrounded by water as if perched on a tiny island makes for an interesting spectacle. But if that footbridge keeps me above the deep water, I welcome it.

On one such floating footbridge, I find Nancy greeting me on the opposite side. She takes pictures of my balancing act; a perfect representation of the true Florida Trail adventure, guts to glory and all.[22] We hike together for a few miles, enjoying the fellowship, and soon arrive at her vehicle, having put in a twenty-one-mile day.

Back home at Nancy's, the high miles transition to

Blissful's new big sister, Nancy, a friend indeed to a hiker in need

rampant hiker hunger. She made dinner ahead of time before coming to retrieve me from the trail, and the delicious beef tips over rice is like ambrosia to a starving hiker. Considering my meals of late from previous backpacking trips, such as fortified ramen noodles (not a good choice, but quick) or some other concoction based on carbs with a little protein thrown in for good measure, the meals I've had at Nancy's are probably what's maintaining my energy level to hike these distances. As the body ages and you demand more from it, adequate

[22] See the book's cover, taken by Nancy in the Nokuse Plantation area on one of those floating footbridges

sources of carbohydrates, veggies, protein, and fats are required. And Nancy's expert cooking is helping well in that department. I haven't eaten this good in weeks.

One final stretch of trail still awaits me before I reach Eglin Air Force Base. Returning to the Nokuse, I'm greeted by more acreage of longleaf pines, with young trees looking like long handle bristle brushes. There are a few more streams to cross before I exit onto the road, and then the main highway to briefly enter Eglin. In the woods is a puffy lichen scattered across the ground called deer moss. The miles go quickly as the trail heads to the main highway, and I see Nancy waiting for me at the trailhead. Today is just thirteen miles, and with a zero day planned tomorrow, it will be good to relax among good company.

*　.　*　.　*

That afternoon I spend with Nancy acclimating to farm life and meeting the animals in residence. I haven't had the opportunity to make their acquaintance, rushing out every day to accomplish the miles that have brought me to the doorstep of Eglin. For now I'm transported from hiker life to farm life. I know nothing about working a farm, even though I grew up in a rural area of upstate New York. We had a few small gardens of vegetables and flowers and some tropical fish, including my very own goldfish named Gloria. Once I even got to babysit a chameleon named Zeb. But we had no other animals on account of family allergies.

I immerse myself into true farm life, complete with Guinea hens racing about, looking for grubs to eat. When I first arrived, I wondered about the strange sound I heard every evening. I thought it must be some kind of alarm going off. Actually it's the Guinea hens talking. They communicate with different sounds depending on if there are strangers nearby. They race about the yard in a flock, and one time Nancy told the story of how the whole flock decided to take a hike down the road to a neighbor's yard. The wild things do have a wandering spirit, as I've seen with the many dogs I've run into on the trail.

The farm is also home to many chickens and two roosters, two horses, three dogs, and cats who mostly hang out on the porch in boxes lined with homemade fleece blankets. The only cat allowed in the house is named P-2. There are two basset hounds, Rusty and Frances, who guard the main house, and another hound mix named Nellie who is trying to decide if she will ever be comfortable with life or not. We all begin a tentative friendship of sorts as the dogs aren't quite sure what to make of me. P-2 is happy to pounce on my lap, lay back, and purr away when I give him a feline massage. I've never been a cat fan, owning dogs the last twenty-five years, but this cat is a sweetie, and I'm in love. But really, I'm falling in love with the simplicity and hard work of farm life.

Nancy now dons old shoes in preparation to feed the horses and chickens. I plan on tagging along as the agricultural student ready to learn how it's done. I've never been near any farm animals except maybe at the county fair. I won't waste a chance to sample something different off-trail and learn what it means to tend the animals that provide eggs, companionship, a good ride in the fields, and which display God's creative touch.

First it's off to feed the horses. The horses can't read a clock, but they stand beside their respective troughs at precisely the right time anyway, tails swishing, heads erect, waiting patiently for their food. We enter the rear of the barn and a small shed where two huge buckets of feed are kept. We mix up both feeds into one concoction with some water and dump it into the respective troughs. The horses love it. The older, maple-colored feller, Nipper, doesn't chew well, so he takes his grand old time eating. The other, an ebony-colored mare named Eva, younger and full of life, gobbles down whatever is there. I find it all fascinating, and after another round of feeding the next day, I'm ready to tackle the chore singlehandedly. Even if I know nothing else about horses, I can feed them. That's one gigantic step above complete ignorance.

Blissful and Eva down on the farm

We move on to greet the chickens. I was introduced to hens before hiking this section of the Florida Trail when I stayed with my writing friend, Lynn. She owns several chickens and showed me the fancy coop they had built—a veritable chicken mansion, with perches for the hens and cubicles for laying eggs. I've never been close to hens nor watched eggs being gathered. Now I observe Nancy enter the coop and take eggs from the cubicles, about half a dozen of them, all different colors with brown and yellow and even blue! The hens seem to know what's coming next like all living creatures when it's feeding time and flock to where she pours feed into a contraption dangling from the ceiling. The chickens peck at it madly. Farm living is fascinating to watch, and I've had a good first day being a part of it all.

* . * . *

The next day I take a zero to rest and give time for the many creeks in the next section of trail to recede after all the rain. Today is February 14, Valentine's Day, and I worry that I might be wearing out my welcome. Nancy appears unconcerned as she takes off for work, leaving me to hold down the farm. I spend the day watching over the animals, greeting all the creatures I made friends with the day before—except the Guinea hens, which shriek when I come near. Even the dogs, who first barked at this strange human wearing some menacing contraption of a backpack, are getting used to me. I also spend time in Nancy's personal ladies cave—a spare room created for her interests that include hiking (she hopes to one day finish the Appalachian Trail), crocheting, reading, and watching television. In fact I watch an Olympic curling match, which reminds me of the bocce I used to play as a kid. Except this is played on ice and uses brooms. Nancy also likes to listen to her favorite musical artists who, to my delight, are also *my* favorite artists. When it came time to drive to the many trailheads this past week, the radio belted out our favorite tunes, and we'd sing along. It's like the good ol' days of young people sharing their favorite songs and artists and what concerts we've attended, of which Nancy has been to many. I'm seeing more and more that this woman God has placed in my life is like a big sister. And as the oldest of three sisters, that's a relationship I've never had.

During the afternoon Papa Bliss and I spend time on a FaceTime video chat where we offer Valentine greetings and exchange small gifts. He sent my gift in the resupply box, along with a big, heart-shaped box of chocolates. I left him a gift bag before heading off for the trail. We then finalize plans for my arrival home. It's hard to believe, but I only have one week left before I finish the Florida Trail. I've been through many adventures since Papa and I started long ago in the Big Cypress National Preserve. It's been an education, a blessing, in trial and triumph, in building oneself up in their most holy faith. One can never have enough experiences in the realm of faith, with each so new and different. Especially on a trail where every day is a venture into the unknown.

Nancy returns from her job to a vase of Valentine flowers from her husband. Then she dives into what she loves best, cooking food for her family. On tonight's menu is shepherd's pie, and it's fabulous. We get to talking like sisters do, and she shows me what it means to live a selfless life devoted to family and living things. Hers is a life well-lived.

But now there's a week of adventure left for me to live with plenty of time to experience life's lessons. In this, the Florida Trail never disappoints.

CHAPTER FIFTEEN

No Ordinary Walk

Eglin Air Force Base and Blackwater River State Forest

Papa Bliss, aka Steve, spent his childhood growing up on air force bases. His father served in the Vietnam War as an air traffic controller, helping planes navigate the busy skies. Even after he left the military, I recalled as a new bride going up in the tower to see my father-in-law hard at work, skillfully giving information to the planes scattered across the radar. Papa Bliss would talk about his life as a kid on base, climbing fences, sneaking past MPs to have fun out of the military zone of influence, all in keeping with the mischievous antics of a boy.

For me, I have no idea what military base living is like or even what it is, except for my brief encounter on the trail as I hiked through Camp Blanding last year. So planning this part of the hike through Eglin Air Force Base is strange to me. It's an active base but also home to some of the most scenic parts of the Florida Trail. How can a base be beautiful, one wonders? I've heard of barracks lined up one after the other, large airfields, hangars. But all that is far distant from where the trail runs along the northern and western boundaries of the base.

Eglin allows hikers to walk through its base, but only if it's open and if you have the proper permit. At different times of the week, the base limits recreational activity for military maneuvers, which is noted on their website. I check the site often that displays a large map, categorized into letters and numbers, and color-coded based on closure status. It's difficult deciphering exactly what numbers and letters correspond to the Florida Trail. It's a guessing game at best, but from what I can tell, a section of the trail is usually closed somewhere in the base the majority of the time. The only exception is a federal holiday weekend, when the entire base is open to the public. And as God would have it—I firmly believe He helps direct our plans, if we let Him—my hike in Eglin is falling right around Presidents' Day weekend. Because this is a federal holiday, I can hike the base without any closures to worry about. With this in mind, I strategically worked out the hike so my time there will coincide with the holiday weekend. It sometimes required me to slow down or speed up, and yes, hike in more difficult situations like major thunderstorms. It all took careful planning. And one thing I like to do is stick to a plan if at all possible. Which is why some hiking days were ten miles or twenty or even zero. It's tough to figure, but it all worked out in the end, which is pretty miraculous. And here I am, right at the start of a holiday weekend.

Nancy drops me off at the Eglin Portal Trailhead where I begin my walk through an unconventional, conventional military base. Papa Bliss is quick to ask me if I see base housing or military personnel roaming about. I see only woods of oaks, pines, and palmettos, scrub brush and flowing streams, and deer moss aplenty scattered across the ground. This may be an active base, but where I am it could be anywhere in some vast wilderness. In the distance is the ominous sound of thunder, and I wonder if a storm is brewing. A quick glance at the cloudless sky reveals the sound is not thunder but bombs going off. Thankfully the noise remains at a distance and there is no thought of ordinance dropping anywhere in my location. I see no military activity around me, no planes, no vehicles or anyone official out on maneuvers. But it hasn't always been that way on past hikes....

Military maneuvers trailside aren't foreign to me. Case in point—the Appalachian Trail near Hawk Mountain in Georgia. In this area, Army Rangers like to conduct maneuvers in the woods right near the trail. Along that route I have sensed someone watching from a concealed foxhole. I even witnessed a helicopter hover in a small valley and soldiers jump out and disappear into the woods. It can be a little nerve-racking, hiking along while hearing the distant boom of bombs or the rat-a-tat-tat sound of automatic rifle fire.

Today though, these Florida woods do their best to make me feel at home and not in enemy territory. I can put aside thoughts of war for peace. Crossing several streams, I observe fresh silt and flattened grass from substantial flooding during the rains. Now I'm glad I took a day off at the farm to allow the area time to dry out. Coming up on Blount Creek, I observe a split log for the crossing, a bit scary if not for the piece of wire acting as handrail. After this I come upon something I never thought I'd see on the Florida Trail—a ladder set against a steep embankment to assist hikers to solid ground. Eglin is not disappointing in the interesting features one can find here.

I head now for Alaqua Creek, one of the most dangerous creek crossings on the trail. Trail maintainers are endeavoring to change that by constructing a sturdy bridge here, and I see a skeleton of one in progress[23]. For

---

[23] I am happy to report as of 2019 the new Alaqua Bridge is now complete and open. The temporary one talked about here has been removed.

a temporary fix, they have strung up a rather interesting means of crossing the creek. Without it I would've been forced to leave Eglin and access roads for many miles. Even if the temporary bridge appears unnerving, I'm thankful it's there. To use it, the hiker must first duck below a wooden beam (not an easy feat carrying a backpack) then cross along plank boards, supported by wire and heavy ropes. The bridge swings nervously like a pendulum. This is definitely not my crossing of choice, and probably one of the scarier moments on a man-made bridge. But I can hardly complain. It's far safer than facing another detour on a dangerous, high speed roadwalk.

Blissful reaches the high point on the Florida Trail, elevation 271 feet. Eglin Air Force Base.

The terrain ahead remains challenging by Florida standards with some actual climbing involved. After hiking on fairly level ground for umpteen amount of miles, any change in elevation is noticeable. But at the top of this particular climb, a sign rewards my effort. The

Florida Trail high point. Elevation...271 feet. Yes, I made it! And yes, I receive snickers from my followers on social media when I post news of my triumph. But hey, small or tall, it's still a huge accomplishment. It means I've hiked close to a thousand miles to get here, so this is nothing to laugh at. It also presents a good contrast of hikes, from an elevation of 271 feet here in Florida to 13,271 feet when I did the Colorado Trail last fall. Each trail and its high points offer great experiences to the hiker. Each has their tough moments, their moments of fascination, interest, and uniqueness. Beauty is in the eye of the beholder, from the stony pinnacles, ponderosa, and wildflowers of the Rockies to the windswept sawgrass, cathedral palms, gnarly oaks, longleaf pine, and swamps of Florida. Each presents challenges and triumph and most importantly, a kinship with others. It is all a part of America the beautiful, with unique treasures to cherish.

That night I make camp at Bull Campsite, a pleasant place complete with benches, a firepit, and plenty of water down the hillside in a gully filled with plants. This site also has the distinction of being the highest campsite on the Florida Trail. I spend a peaceful night there, only to realize there aren't many more nights like these left before I'll reach the end of my journey. It seems hard to believe the end is near.

A few raindrops come calling overnight but nothing major, and I hike out early for a good eighteen-mile jaunt through the heart of Eglin. I reach yet another milestone, the 1,000-mile mark on the trail and just a little over a hundred miles left to finish. The trail skirts a vast area of logged land and prescribed burning as I follow tiny orange flags through it with the words FLORIDA TRAIL written on them. The area will one day revert to wilderness, but it shows how much the terrain can change. I pass over more nice bridges and boardwalks when suddenly I see a familiar face eating lunch by the side of the trail. It's none other than my big sister Nancy, out for her own six-mile walk to Walton Pond. We hop over each other as we head west and along a flood plain that shows off the lingering effects of standing water and mud from all the flooding. At a major creek crossing, I stop to get water for the night. Nancy arrives shortly after to help me filter and even carry water for me. She fills the hole of a friend indeed to one in need, as she has for nearly a week now.

Arriving at Walton Pond, a camping area that caters to car campers, we meet a cheery guy who asks if I'm hiking the Florida Trail. It's nice to hear from one who knows of the trail's existence and best of all, who celebrates it. I tell him I am indeed hiking it, and he rewards me with a bottle of cold water. I enjoy it while he and Nancy chatter away about hiking and trails. Nancy and I then continue up the trail to find a good spot to camp. I bid her good night until tomorrow when she will pick me up for another night's stay at the farm. I look forward to seeing the family and the animal crew. They're my trail family now through this part of the Panhandle.

The next morning, boardwalks greet me along with day hikers wandering about. The sight of other hikers on the trail surprises me, as I've seen very little in the way of anyone out here. I'm not certain if it's because they don't know the Florida Trail exists or Floridians prefer the ocean and lakes. Except for encountering seven backpackers, a few day hikers in the Econfina Section, the three Paisley angels and folks walking the paved paths of Lake Okeechobee, it's been a lonely trail. Which can be good for solitude but bad for those who want people to know about it and help maintain it.

Today the trail dumps me onto a road heading north to the thriving metropolis of Crestview. The trail in Eglin is incomplete because of a major obstacle, the Yellow River. Since there's no way to cross the river at this point, the trail must detour onto roads through town to access a bridge before dipping back to meet the Yellow River basin. But the heart of Crestview allows hikers to take advantage of all that a town stop has to offer, like lodging and resupplying at the grocery stores, and for me, not one but two lunches at fast food restaurants. I proceed through town and then on to where my big sister trail angel is waiting for me at a gas station.

It's good to be back home on the farm for a quick overnight. I greet the animals I've come to know and love—the basset hounds Rusty and Frances, the neurotic hound Nellie, P-2 the cat, the chickens, and the Guinea hens who continue their strange chattering. And of course the horses, Nipper and Eva, for whom I quickly accept the role of horse feeder after learning the ropes from Nancy the last time I was here. I honestly think I could do some of this farming deal one day. As a kid I used to dream about raising sheep. Maybe it's in my future. One never knows.

That evening we visit the lonely mule across the street and an eccentric neighbor who spills out the woes of the neighborhood—it seems every place, even out in the country, has its bad eggs—and I find civilization far more unsettled and stressed. A backpacker experiences peace in the quiet wilderness, but this wilderness adventure is rapidly drawing to a close. Later on I track the river stage for my next wander along the Yellow River basin to find it elevated because of past rains but not enough to cause concern. I've repacked the backpack with food for the next section, and everything is set for my final return to the Florida Trail.

The following morning, energized by cheese toast and words of wisdom from Nancy about the next section, I head out for my final days on the trail. The next time I will see my big sister Nancy, it will be at the northern terminus of the Florida Trail at Fort Pickens. It's difficult to believe.

I venture along yet another roadwalk, which is fairly pleasant as roads go, with limited cars and a wide shoulder to walk on. In some parts there are even powerline easements that afford a bit of hiking privacy off the beaten path. After crossing Interstate 10, which I haven't seen since the town of Madison long ago, and wandering down some dirt roads, I enter Blackwater River State Forest. This area lies close to the Yellow River floodplain where the water has yet to fully recede, making for soggy shoes. It's a good thing my feet are trail-hardened by all the walking and the water that are part of the perpetual Florida Trail lifestyle. One does adapt with the mental attitude that says: *Wet feet and swamp walking are a part of a unique experience. There are always things to see and learn and enjoy on any kind of a trek, including this one.*

The trail guide is not quite clear about if there could be hazards with the stream crossings in this section, especially with water levels running high due to rain. When I reach the first stream, I see a simple log thrown across for good measure. Logs and I don't get along very well. They are often slippery, and I envision falling off into the water. So this first crossing I take slowly, one step at a time, holding the razor thin metal wire of a handrail for balance, feeling like a trapeze artist crossing the great and dangerous void with no net to catch me. I hop off, none the worse, and continue on until the next one, similar in configuration with a hewed log and a wire handrail for balance. At least I'm more confident. The crossing is made in relative ease, and I happily bounce off, only to hear a distinct stirring of leaves right in front of me.

I stop, look, and there before me is a big, dark snake. He shimmies his tail back and forth in the leaves to create a sound, his body coiled, his gaping mouth baring some impressive fangs. I jump back, expecting at any moment for the thing to strike. But he lays there coiled, his mouth wide open, not moving a reptilian muscle. If only I had the nerve to take a picture—it would have been a one in a million shot. But I value safety more and take a picture from behind. I can clearly see the triangular-shaped head, a telltale sign of a poisonous snake. Later I realize I'd stumbled upon a cottonmouth. A cottonmouth has characteristics like what I witnessed: the sound it makes in the leaves to warn its enemies, the coiling, the gaping white mouth displaying fangs as a deterrent—hence the name cottonmouth. They enjoy hanging out in boggy, wet areas, so this is prime habitat. It's strange I've never seen them anywhere else, with the many boggy areas I've traipsed through. The encounter makes me wary about future stream crossings. When I reach the final stream where I plan to gather water for the night, yet another cottonmouth scurries away, making two encounters in one day.

At least the campsite tonight remains calm with no intruders except for a brief rain shower. I sleep well and awaken to finish this section of trail. But I wander through a forest hammock with a smoky haze in the air. Something is burning somewhere nearby, a prescribed burn in full swing. I stop and check the websites on my phone to see if there are any active burns but come up empty. Of course that doesn't mean something isn't going on within the state forest boundary where I'm hiking. I remain vigilant, hoping I'm not stumbling into an active burn. That actually happened to a Florida Trail hiker who got caught in the middle of a burn and needed to be rescued. The forest service often forgets a trail runs through these woods and that folks are out hiking it. I faced a fresh burn back in the Apalachicola National Forest, and although there was still tape up to warn would-be hikers, there was no other sign of activity except for a the pungent odor and fresh charcoal-colored ground. Prescribed burns, as I've talked about in this book, are a reality of hiking the trail, and the hiker must do all they can to find out when the burns will take place. Hopefully in the future there will be better coordination with planned burns and hikers, or perhaps burning can be avoided during the main hiking season of December through March.

At last I walk out of the smoke-filled area to see a mileage sign at a major trail junction. When one comes upon any sign out here, it's a good reason to stop. On this sign, one way points to Fort Pickens (the first time I've seen the name of the trail's northern terminus) the other to Alabama. Some hikers take the Blackwater Trail route to Alabama where they can then connect to the Pinhoti Trail and even the Appalachian Trail. But I will follow the orange blazes of the Florida Trail that now heads south and west to Gulf Islands National Seashore and the northern terminus, a mere fifty-five miles away. I snap a picture of the sign and revel in the short distance remaining, recollecting the joy and excitement I felt on the Appalachian Trail when a sign in Maine pointed out fifty miles to the northern terminus at Katahdin. After so many miles and likewise, many adventures, it's hard to imagine this hike will soon be wrapping up.

Exiting the Blackwater State Forest, I once more drop onto a bustling highway for a short roadwalk over the Yellow River. At the corner sits a friendly convenience store where I load up on all the junk food one should never ingest in life or risk cardiac failure—like hotdogs, donuts, Doritos, and lemonade. But boy, it's good. With all that sugar and fat, I feel like I can do anything, except what's ahead of me—a massive work zone to create a new bridge spanning the Yellow River. I tentatively head for the site, wondering where I'm supposed to walk, with cones showing cars where to go but no shoulder to speak of. I pass a construction vehicle and inquire of the two men hanging out, jawing with each other, and ask where I should walk. The one who appears to be more of a head honcho tells me to stay in the construction area behind the cones. I look at this suggestion rather dubiously, as the only cones on my left are where construction guys in their hard hats are working with a massive machine that's making a loud plinking noise. But I charge ahead and stay behind the cones as instructed, passing workers on the bridge laying down materials for the new highway. No one seems to care I'm walking through their work site, even past the huge machine acting like a massive hammer to knock metal beams into the riverbed of the Yellow River. It's an ear-shattering chunk, chunk sound, and I plug my ears with my fingers as I pass by. I've never had the privilege of walking through a busy highway construction site like this, and it's another checkmark off the list of new hiking experiences.

After the construction zone, I look to my right and see two orange blazes painted on the wildlife fence and feel a sense of relief. Heading down the very steep embankment to the base of the fence, I follow the blazing until I reach another set of double blazes. And here the trail stops. I peer now through fencing that is completely closed off to access. I'm standing there, staring at this obstruction before me and wondering what to do, when a construction guy wanders over and asks if I need help. I tell him I'm looking for the Florida Trail, but the way is blocked. Like most here in the state, he stares at me rather blankly until he says many hikers just follow the fencing down to the road there (or *thar*, as he has a southern twang). I try doing what he suggests but get bogged down by thick brush and weeds that make the way impossible. I return to the closed fence and double blazes, noting how the fencing ends in a boggy area. I'm thinking I might just scoot around the fence and take my chance crossing the bog to reach the trail in the woods.

I'm about ready to embark on my plan when another construction worker calls down to me in the ravine from the main highway above. He shakes his head when I relate my plan and says in another stiff accent, "Thar's cottonmouths a 'plenty in thar." I shudder, remembering all too well my encounters yesterday. He then says I need come back up to "this here road" and head down to "that thar road a spell" and go find it "somewheres." After deciphering his very thick southern accent, I determine he wants me to come back up the hill to the main highway and head down to the next road intersection. But first I have to climb up the near-vertical embankment. The worker above has to give me a helping hand to drag me up the final part. My hat goes off to the friendly workers who assisted a middle-aged hiker in navigating this latest struggle on the trail.

I check my map app on my phone, but it doesn't cover my momentary detour, so I take a gamble that the next road I come to will lead me to the trail. And like clockwork, after about a mile or so, I intersect the orange blazes coming out of the woods and immeasurable relief pours over me. I stop for a snack and water, glad I'm back on the trail.

Suddenly out of nowhere, a guy on a motorcycle zooms by me, riding directly on the trail. I stare at this scene in shock and dismay, wondering how far he is going. I ends up following miles of tire ruts on the trail, chewed by this guy's cycle. Very depressing to say the least. But soon I leave the remnants of the awful scene behind for an interesting steephead ravine and a fine view overlooking the drainage area of Weaver Creek. I'm immersed once more in the beauty of Eglin Air Force Base in this picturesque stream and take time to gather water for tonight's campsite.

Now the trail crosses back over the major highway, and once again I note more wildlife fencing. But this time there's a "door" in the fenceline to let hikers in, near a kiosk with trail information. I camp soon after that, dead tired after a twenty-one-mile day but happy to find a place to spend the night. It's hot and sticky, and I can hear cars out on the highway and bugs revving up around my tentsite. But it's also my final night in my tent on the Florida Trail and a time of contemplation and reflection over all I've seen, the challenges I've endured, and the knowledge that I've come this far. I lie in my tent thinking about tomorrow and what's ahead the next few days—a place of sand and wind where I have no experience backpacking, and the final push to finish this 1,100-mile journey.

CHAPTER SIXTEEN

THE WIND AND THE SAND CALL MY NAME

THE SEASHORE

I honestly didn't expect to feel melancholic when facing the final days of an adventure that began long ago in a swamp, but I am. I leave behind the old of the unique Florida woods to embrace a new walk. That means saying farewell to the longleaf pine, the palmettos and palm trees, the gnarly oak reminiscent of Fangorn Forest from *Lord of the Rings*, and of course the cypress trees and knobby cypress knees. I will exchange raw Florida wilderness for sand and wind and water which to many symbolize the real Florida they know and love. No more tenting by palmettos or in pine forests. With the mileage and lack of camping in this part, I will be hoteling it from here on in.

And so begins my foray into civilization. I exit Eglin Air Force Base and the forests that have brought much beauty and pleasure and hike along a major highway heading toward Navarre and the Gulf of Mexico. Whenever I walk a road, I often wonder what drivers speeding along in their cars think when they see some figure carrying a backpack, trudging along the side of the road. Are they happy they aren't in my shoes, carrying all that weight? Are they wishing they *were* in my shoes and not spending another day cooped up in the office? Are they worried about a lone woman out there, or wondering how I can do such a thing in the first place without getting scared or crazy or injured or exhausted? Little do they know, but I have gone through all of these emotions and more. I've been scared. I sometimes think a long-distance hike into the unknown is a crazy idea. I've suffered many injuries on my hikes, but thankfully on this hike it's been limited, except for the bad toes and the bout with a respiratory infection early on. I do feel exhausted, probably from hiking continuously for six weeks, and now I look forward to finishing the trail in style.

Today is an eight-and-a-half-mile hike to a hotel where I plan to spend the night. The miles go by quickly with the terrain converted to a cityscape, sprinkled with shops and businesses. My first stop is a store on the corner where I nab a cold drink and some snacks to tide me over. Tomorrow is slated to be a big mile day to Pensacola Beach, hiking on a beach for twenty miles, so I cherish the half day of rest. On the way to the hotel, I see Santa Rosa Sound before me and the bridge leading to the barrier island of Navarre Beach, which becomes part of Gulf Islands National Seashore, and finally the Gulf of Mexico itself. When I passed through the St. Marks National Wildlife Refuge a few weeks back, I glimpsed faint palm trees framing the Gulf of Mexico. It seemed so near but still so far. Now I'm knocking on the door and soon to hike beside its waves and water come morning.

Right now, though, a barbecue restaurant catches my hungry hiker eye, and I stop in for an early feast. The hike transitions to beach time with a full chicken barbecue and all the fixings and a pretty view overlooking the bay. It does feel strange seeing sand and water after being in woods and walking on roads for so long. The feeling follows me that afternoon when I sit out in a beach chair behind the hotel, gazing at the water sparkling in the sun and thinking how much this looks and feels like the Florida everybody recognizes. But I have seen and walked the real Florida, to places people rarely see, encountering the beauty and challenge that goes along with it, and I feel quite fortunate.

I break for some laundry duty and fall into company with a woman named Melissa. She's a wanderer like me but living from motel to motel. We get to talking, one thing leads to another, and I share about my hike and how I do what I do in life by believing and trusting in God. It becomes another God moment for me on the trail, and when I ask if I can pray for her circumstances, she agrees. To me this is a side of the big picture I often overlook. It's not just about me walking a trail. It's a journey of faith and hope and pointing to the One who cares for all of us. He is our Provider in times of need, even in the darkness and the challenges and the good times. He is in the forefront of all we do. He is our all in all. And He will see me through to the end.

* . * . *

It's early to bed, early to rise for the planned twenty-miler today. This will be my first backpacking experience on a beach, and I have no idea how hot it might get with no shade available. I'm a bit concerned too as the one place that's supposed to have water, Opal Beach, may not be open. So I leave at dawn to cross the bridge over Santa Rosa Sound, just in time to see the sun rising in the east. I'm delighted my departure coincides with this spectacle as I head toward the barrier island and Navarre Beach. With the sun shining strong, it's not long before I feel the heat radiating off the pavement beneath my feet. I liberally apply sunscreen and don sunglasses and a hat. Another issue that crops up is the lack of bathroom facilities. There's not a tree or what-have-you to duck behind, either. I happen upon a portable toilet sitting at a beach house construction site and ask the lone guy there in a truck if I can use it. He shrugs and says it's nothing to him, and so I do, happy I thought to ask. I realize I do things on a hike I'd never think of back home, like using a construction site privy. It goes along with the life of a hiker.

The trail exits the highway at the entrance to Gulf Islands National Seashore to begin a lengthy trek along the beach paralleling the Gulf Coast. Earlier on the trail route, I encountered sandy areas, especially in Big Cypress. This is my first experience backpacking on a sandy beachfront. Which means full sun, no shade, feet sinking into sand and then having to lift feet out of it, sand getting in your face, fierce sunlight, and sunglasses smeared by sea spray. It's desert walking at its best, and it requires some changes in the way one does this hike as well as coping with the mental challenges. The constant sinking and lifting of feet out of the sand soaks up more energy and muscle, quickly exhausting me. With the big mile day planned to the town of Pensacola Beach, I need to conserve what strength I have. I look for places where the sand is hard packed and easy to walk on so I don't sink. For a while I follow another set of footprints that appears to be hiking those hardened places. I pass large sand dunes, sea gulls and other birds wandering about the shore, and listen to the talking waves. The water here is a pleasant shade of blue, the sand an attractive pearly white. I've spent many summers at the Outer Banks of North Carolina, but the water here looks and acts differently, with a nautical character all its own.

I also become a beachcomber as I search for interesting shells to bring back to Papa Bliss. In college Papa spent a fall semester in St. Croix, developing a fondness for treasures of the sea while sailing and scuba diving. He texted me earlier this day, asking if I could bring home something interesting from the seashore. I find a few perfect scallop shells and then a partial sand dollar. Later I realize this area is rich in sand dollars, stirring up memories of my parents rising at six A.M. to look for sand dollars on the shores of Edisto Beach in South Carolina. They would return to our RV in triumph just as we awoke, with a hard sought-after, precious sand dollar in their possession. Although the one I find here is but

Beach backpacking for the first time

a half chunk of a sand dollar, it's still good, and I put it away for safekeeping.

Now I look with eagerness for shade and water as I arrive at Opal Beach. To my glee the restrooms are open and water is available. I seek shade in one of the many picnic shelters, drink lots of water, eat food, and contemplate what's ahead. So far it hasn't been terribly hot, for which I'm thankful. The navigation has been a straight shot along the coast, and it's going well.

But then the trail leaves the beach and enters a marshland. I lose the trail completely, relying on my map app to direct me here and there. When I locate the white posts embedded in the sand, with faded orange blazes painted on them, I realize now why I had a tough time finding the trail. White posts are difficult to spot against the light-colored sand, intermixed with the sun's glare. I'm glad I'm on the official trail though as there are several bridges to carry the hiker over some soggy bogs. Steep dunes in the area, sporting vegetation and even a few oaks, provide shade in this section. The dunes are impressive and even make for some climbing. I then pass the only place where hikers can camp on the national seashore—Bayview Campsite, with no drinkable water anywhere and likely to have its share of insects with the close proximity to the bay. I'm glad I planned to stay at a hotel in Pensacola Beach. Hiking out here all day in the sand and sun, along with the miles, is wiping me out. It's been a long, hot, tough day. When I finally exit the marshland, the trail parallels the road heading past tall condominiums that mark the beginning of Pensacola Beach and my rest stop for the night. The sun begins its retreat toward the horizon when I finally arrive at the hotel—tired, beat up, foot sore, but exuberant.

The cheery clerk at the front desk is eager to hear about my adventures, particularly the Appalachian Trail, never mind that I'm nearing the conclusion of the 1,100-

mile Florida Trail which is pretty important to me. He gives me a nice large room in the rear of the hotel, away from the cars speeding along the highway. The nearby restaurant becomes the place to toast my final day with rum punch, a hamburger, and deep fried green beans. Yes indeed, tomorrow's *the* Day. The End Game. Or End Day. It's difficult to believe yet always the goal before me when I began this trek. With this trail being one of my longer ventures outside the Appalachian Trail, there's plenty to reflect on and great anticipation for the final day's walk to Fort Pickens.

* \. * \. *

An oversized beach ball in the morning can't help but put one in a celebratory mood as I leave early to hike in the cool of the day. The streets of Pensacola Beach are quiet. I gaze at the acres of empty parking lots surrounding a water tower painted to look like a beach ball and think how glad I am to be coming through at this time. I chose to end my hike in late February, well before the spring break crowds. Passing Jimmy Buffet's Margaritaville Hotel, which looks more like a ghost town with only a few cars in the parking lot, I can say there are no banners waving or folks tooting horns to add to the excitement of my final day on the Florida Trail. I'll toot my own horn, I suppose, with plenty of reflection as I exit the town and head into Fort Pickens.

Fort Pickens on the Gulf Islands National Seashore is a system of forts put into place in the 1800s to protect Pensacola Bay and the navy shipyard from enemy attack. Within the historic area are the remnants of forts, along with a visitor center and public campground. Just before the entrance station, the Florida Trail swings back to the beach where again I pick and choose where to walk in the wind-driven, sinking sand that also forms dunes. This barren land, with little evidence of human habitation except for the park road and the occasional buzz of cars, is a fitting place to ponder the end of a long journey. I've been blessed to experience the true Florida wilderness like the explorers and pioneers who came before me, some looking for treasure, others for a new life, away from the oppression of their native land. The interior of the state along the trail offered glimpses into unique habitats in the palmettos and pines and oaks and swamps. This area of wide beaches reminds me of what it must have looked like for those arriving to the New World—the white sand sprinkled with seashells and beachgrass waving a greeting or for me, a final farewell.

I've been in similar situations when ready to finish a long-distance hiking trail, and each has been memorable. On the final day of the Long Trail of Vermont, I was the sole person standing at the sign, wondering who would take my picture, when a hiker just happened to come by and take the celebratory photo. So it was at Waterton Canyon on the Colorado Trail as again I arrived alone, completing a 480-mile journey, only to have a couple riding bikes agree to take my picture. I do miss Papa Bliss, as he has been with me on several of my finishes—the Allegheny Trail of West Virginia and my southbound hike of the Appalachian Trail that concluded in Harper's Ferry. I did ask, or rather begged him to come down and walk these final days with me on the Florida Trail. After all, it began with him in the Big Cypress National Preserve, through the mosquito-infested canal walk, around Lake Okeechobee and to our bungalow for Christmas. Sadly, he was unable to make it.

But God provides. When I exit the beach by an interesting battery formation, I find the cheerful face of my new big sister, Nancy. She's arrived to walk the final stretch with me. As we head through the campground with folks lazily sitting beside their huge RVs, no one knows or cares what is about to happen—that a lone hiker is about to finish an amazing journey. We exit the campground and head to another park nature trail where Nancy informs me the end is near. I'm glad she's with me.

The finish at the northern terminus of the Florida Trail!
Fort Pickens, Gulf Islands National Seashore

If I were doing this alone, I probably would have passed by the modest marker, and the whole end would have felt anticlimactic.

Instead Nancy makes it a momentous occasion, hurrying ahead as I stride across the bridge where several visitors are looking at this strange display of a hiker being videoed walking up and over the bridge. And there on the other side of the bridge is the modest monument marking the northern terminus of the Florida Trail. Like other accomplishments of traildom, of which this is a biggie for me, I kneel and give God the glory and honor and thanks for His protection, His provision, and His mighty angels that have seen me finish another hiking trail. Nancy cheers and we exchange hugs. We then walk out to her car to deposit my backpack before heading over to the Fort Pickens gift shop to register the conclusion of the hike. Nancy already informed the ladies there I'd be finishing today. They have out the colorful butterfly notebook with for me to sign with the words "I finished!" and offer their congratulations. All I can think is, *Wow*.

The Florida Trail is done. One thousand, one hundred miles of adventure.

Yet the emotion of it all is only beginning to sink in....

CHAPTER SEVENTEEN

REFLECTIONS OF AN ADVENTURE WELL-LIVED

I'm now basking in farm life once more with Nancy and the animals before my flight for home the next day. I feed the horses, Nipper and Eva, with confidence. To P-2 and the other cats, the chickens, the Guinea hens, Nellie, the wild and wacko hound, and the beloved basset hounds Rusty and Frances I say hello. I greet Nancy's husband and her son. I'm part of the family now, as I've been with them ten days. I've learned a great deal. But it draws to an end when Nancy takes me to the airport for my flight home. I must transition from life in the wilderness back to civilization. There's time now to think about the experience and cherish the memories.

Having completed the Florida Trail, without a doubt the Panhandle section is my favorite. For the hiker who only wants to sample a few weeks on the Florida Trail, the Panhandle offers a fascinating journey of rivers and limestone, of a wildlife refuge, titi swamps with towering cypress trees, long needle pine forests and cathedral palms, to the experience of the seashore. It offers hikers a unique and interesting journey through the wilderness that is native Florida in all its glory. Even if the way is sprinkled with roadwalks and hiker dogs to add to the adventure.

Hiking the Florida Trail showed me that this state is not just beaches and tourist attractions. Its charm lies in the fascinating ecosystems of flora and fauna like no other place in the United States. I enjoyed seeing the many variety of birds, the gators, turtles, even the cottonmouths. A forest hammock or a cypress dome or cypress strand or even cypress knee groves display both the unusual and the beautiful. Longleaf pine forests, cathedral palms, and forest floors thick with palmettos show off the fascinating plant life of the region. It reminds me of an island paradise where one doesn't have to fly to Tahiti to walk among towering pine and palms or set up a tent among the palmettos. One doesn't have to venture far to find flat terrain, yes, but terrain that still challenges with walks in water, pulling a limb out of sucking mud, or performing a balancing act on a slick log or bog bridge. And who can forget the roadwalks that display Americana and the generation of settlers from long ago, revealing true Floridian character far removed from beaches and Walt Disney World.

The Florida Trail is part of the National Scenic Trail System, and 2018 marked the fiftieth anniversary of the National Trail System. Hikers are well aware of the popular trails such as the Appalachian Trail and the Pacific Crest Trail. The Florida Trail is a welcome addition with its diversity in plant life and wildlife unlike any other. Of course one can climb many a mountain for a fine view. But the view of a sawgrass prairie that conjures up images of Africa or gazing up into tall palm trees reminiscent of a Pacific isle, or seeing a tiny glade of cypress knees that looks like an elfin kingdom puts the Florida Trail in a class by itself. And therefore, it's a must-hike trail. If hikers are looking for adventure when winter closes in, when the wind and cold and snow makes hiking inaccessible, unpleasant, or even dangerous, the Florida Trail beckons with a winter hiking experience unlike any other.

Of course, I would be remiss if I didn't point out the greatest part of Florida's charm. Its inhabitants. People who go out of their way to help hikers in times of need. From taking my injured husband to his car, to inviting me into their homes, to giving money from a paycheck, to picking me up from a train ride or allowing me to become a part of the family, the people I meet will always be the highlight of any hike. Every time I go out, I think it will be nature, or a view, or the hike itself that refreshes my soul. But it's the heart of people that speaks louder than any view or quiet solitude at a campsite. People who make an adventure real. People who give of themselves in so many ways. This is what I take away most from my hiking and why I yearn for more. That in the kindness of people in strange places, we also see the kindness of a living God who cares about us. He wants us to know Him in the deepest parts of our lives and in the journey we each take. In the end, it's not the journey that matters. The miles hiked. Or how quickly we did those miles. Or standing at the end of a journey at the final monument. All of that is fleeting. What matters most are the lessons learned and what we can then bring from the experience to help others.

So by all means, take a hike. Enjoy an adventure. And while you're at it, go hike the Florida Trail. Like I said from the beginning...you'll never be the same. And that's a good thing.

APPENDIX OF FLORIDA TRAIL HELPS

The Florida Trail Guide:
www.floridahikes.com

Florida Trail Association:
www.floridatrail.org

Blissful Hiking (my blog):
www.blissfulhiking.com

Guthooks Florida Trail map app for your phone:
www.atlasguides.com

Facebook Groups on the Florida Trail

ACKNOWLEDGMENTS

With special thanks to:

Steve "Papa Bliss" who was there when it all began and there emotionally and spiritually all the way to the end

Sandra Friend, co-author of *The Florida Trail Guide*, for all her help, encouragement, and yes, reminding me it's not Great Cypress but Big Cypress

My critiquers, Steve and Susan: Many thanks

David and Roseanna White and WhiteFire Publishing: for taking a chance on another trail book and for keeping me hiking

To Nancy and the Frey family: thanks is not enough

And thanks to the many trail angels who helped me along the way:

"Chuck Norris and Tigger," "Dovetail" and Mom Weber, Christina Y, Chase, Tom Kennedy, Mike Gormley, "Trucker Bob," "Trail Talker" and the Paisley Angels, "Hammock Hanger," Janie Hamilton, Lynn and Paul Coleman, Randy and Melissa Madison, Robert Sutherland, those angels along the roadwalks who reached out to me and who shuttled Papa Bliss, and the followers on social media for their thoughts (some hilarious) and prayers

To God be the Glory

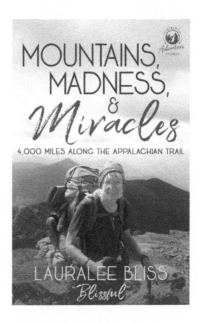

Mountains, Madness, & Miracles:
4,000 Miles Along the Appalachian Trail

In this look into a lifelong dream of adventure, Blissful reflects on the 4,000 mile journey she undertook with her teen son, hiking the Appalachian Trail from Georgia to Maine, and then again from Maine to Georgia as a solo hiker.